THE
FRANKLIN
FI

THE
FRANKLIN
FI

A PERSONAL FINANCE ADVENTURE
FOR NEXT GENERATION INVESTORS

BOOK 1

Shane Dillon

LOGICAL JOURNEY PUBLISHING

If you could travel back in time,
what would you tell your
sixteen-year-old self?

Contents

Introduction

The nod, the nod, oh the horror of the nod! You know what I am talking about. That state between sleep and consciousness in which the only thing keeping you awake is the nod of your head. I was no stranger to sleeping in class, but this early into the school year was an all-time low for me. I was in biology class and we were watching some boring video on bacteria. Mr. Heartwood, my biology teacher, insisted on starting the semester with bacteria because it is the simplest form of life. What did I care about bacteria? My dream was to be a stockbroker on Wall Street.

I was doomed from the get-go. It was freaking hot in the classroom, and I was tired from waking up early. The lights were out so we could watch the boring video on bacteria. I kept telling myself that I was just daydreaming. But who was I kidding? Daydreaming always leads to a full-on nap. At this point, the only thing keeping me awake was the occasional nod of my head. Why is it so hard to keep your head balanced while trying to sleep upright? I was riding the edge between sleep and consciousness when it hit me. I remembered thinking before I dozed off: "I don't think anybody will notice if I hunt some zzz's right quick, just a few minutes. It will feel so good." You've been there before! Don't lie!

Then boom-shaka-laka, I was out. Hunting zzzeason had begun.

The next thing I knew, I was awake and on the trading floor of the New York Stock Exchange. What the heck! How did all of these stockbrokers and traders get here? From all sides, I was surrounded by people shouting and shoving me. Buy! Sell! Buy! Sell!

"Buy 100,000 shares of Voka Computers at $152.34 per share!" a stockbroker screamed.

"Sell, sell 300,000 shares of Doctor and Ramble at $85.23 per share. No, no! What are you doing? Sell, sell!!!" another said in a panic.

I looked around and thought to myself: "How in the world did I get here? Am I some sort of stockbroker or stock trader?" Then I decided I needed to figure out real quick if this was real or just a dream. So, I lightly shoved the guy next to me in his shoulder.

"Hey, watch it buddy!" He barked at me and shoved me back even harder. Oh yeah, it's real!

Then involuntarily I cried out, "Buy 500,000 shares of Duka Motors at $49.29 per share."

This was the moment I had prepared for my whole life. I had made it to the big leagues. I was a stockbroker on the New York Stock Exchange. In my left hand, I was holding a handful of buy and sell tickets. In my right hand, I had a pencil for filling out the order slips. Duka Motors had finally dipped below $50 per share and based on my valuations, I knew it was worth twice that. I couldn't miss with Duka Motors. They had cornered the autonomous, solar-powered car market and their assets alone were worth $100 per share. It was just my luck there was a dip in the stock's price because of a minor problem with the car's battery. A battery had blown up and had nearly killed the driver. The news of the explosion scared away practically all of the other investors. When it dipped below $50 a share, I knew it had hit rock bottom.

My original order of 500,000 shares was filled at an average price of $49.87 per share. I had taken a $25 million position in Duka Motors and I was just getting started. The stock price ticked up over $50 per share, so I decided to buy another 500,000 shares. I knew it was only a matter of time before the stock price took off and I didn't want to be late to the party. I now had over $50 million invested in Duka Motors.

The order hit and filled within the hour. I had just taken a huge stake in Duka and now all I could do was sit back and let the market work its magic.

Apparently, the word got around the street that I had taken a position in Duka Motors. Once that happens, the copycat investors come out to play—which is like adding gasoline to a bonfire. Everybody on Wall Street knew Franklin Fi had the hot hand, and the copycats were quick to follow my investments. Once the copycat investors started buying up shares in Duka, the price took off! As other buyers flooded the market, Duka's stock price was driven up 8% over the course of the day. I made an easy $4 million in one trading session. It was true, I was the "can't miss kid" and everybody on Wall Street knew it. When Franklin Fi takes a position, the street soon follows.

Next thing I knew, money started raining down from the heavens. Piles of one-hundred-dollar bills were stacking up everywhere. I started jumping up and down in the piles of money like they were puddles of water. I screamed, "I'm the 'can't-miss kid!'" All the while, I was heaving handfuls of hundred-dollar bills into the air. Music started to play and scenes of wealth started to pass before my eyes. I was no longer on a trading floor. Instead, I was magically floating through the air, enabling me to observe my life of luxury from above.

Hey, that's me throwing out the first pitch at a Yankees game.

Wait! Is that me in a bright red Ferrari rolling down Fifth Avenue? How did that happen?

Private jet.

Beach house.

Magnum bottles of champagne being sprayed everywhere.

Next thing I knew I was pulling up to what appeared to be my chateau. What the heck?! How did I end up in France? The front gates read, "Chateau Franklin." I pulled my bright red Ferrari through the gates, just as my butler was running out to greet me and park my car. I throw him the keys...

Brrring!!! Brrring!!! Brrring!!!
Brrring!!! Brrring!!! Brrring!!!

Wait, that's not how the closing bell of the New York Stock Exchange sounds. The closing bell on the floor of the stock market sounds more like a ding-ding-ding-ding sound. And this is a Brrring!!! Brrring!!! Brrring!!! Brrring!!! Brrring!!! Brrring!!! What's this? Where am I?

No, it can't be. That's a freaking school bell! Why is the school bell ringing at my chateau? Wait! Where is my chateau? What happened to my butler and the bright red Ferrari?

Who or what keeps hitting my shoulder? No, no, no!

That's the school bell. And the thumping on my shoulder is my classmates rushing out of the classroom, hitting me one by one with their backpacks as they pass by me.

Eww. There is wet stuff on my cheek. Is that drool? I am back at my desk in Mr. Heartwood's biology class. The summer heat hits me like a ton of bricks. My sweaty shirt is stuck to my chest and I am slumped over my desk in a pool of drool. It's the same old desk I had tagged earlier with my pen. Brilliantly, I wrote "BIOLOGY SUCKS!" on the desk. Little did I know, it had been transferred to my forehead. It read:

BIOLOGY SUCKS

Out of instinct, I jumped up and yelled, "I'M AWAKE, I'M AWAKE, MOM, LEAVE ME ALONE, I'M AWAKE, I'LL BE RIGHT DOWN FOR BREAKFAST, LEAVE ME ALONE!" It was epic, I jumped up deliriously with an inked forehead screaming, "MOM, LEAVE ME ALONE, I'M AWAKE."

"Mr. Franklin Fi, it's going to be a long semester. I know it is hot, but that is no excuse," Mr. Heartwood told me. "I'll let it slide this time. Just don't let it happen again. Now, get your bag and get out of here before you're late for your next class. Sheesh! Kids these days!"

Embarrassed, I snatched my biology book off of my desk and ran out of the classroom. What a disaster!

1

Dreams of a Stockbroker

My name is Franklin Fi, and I am a sixteen-year-old who is obsessed with the stock market. Maybe that is why I dream about it all of the time.

The one and only goal I have in life is to work on Wall Street. As long as I can remember (last week), all I have ever wanted to be is a stockbroker and to make millions of dollars. I don't ask for much, just to be young and rich!

Someone once told me, if you write down your dreams in a notebook, they will come true. Sounds easy enough to me. So instead of paying attention in class, I just sit there and write in my notebook, "I, Franklin Fi, want to be a stockbroker when I grow up. I, Franklin Fi, want to be a stockbroker when I grow up." Okay, I think you get the point.

I know you are probably thinking, it is pretty ridiculous for a sixteen-year-old from St. Louis, Misery to declare such things…oops, I mean St. Louis, Missouri. But it is my dream and I want the whole universe to know it. I fill up notebook after notebook with my dreams, convinced that one day they will come true.

Ever since I started reading Baron Wufot's newsletter, I have been obsessed with the stock market and personal finance. You see, Baron Wufot is the richest man in the solar system. Like me, he grew up in the state of Missouri, but not in St. Louis. He grew up and still lives in our state's capital, Jefferson City. Baron Wufot created his newsletter for teens to teach them about investing and how to be successful in life. He doesn't make any money from his newsletter. I suspect he quit caring about how much money he makes a long time ago. It seems to me his goal now is to help the youth of the world.

His newsletter is where I have picked up most of my knowledge about the stock market. Based on the newsletter, Baron Wufot is tired of seeing the youth of the country continuously fall into debt. It's a vicious cycle. Most of us will go on to graduate high school, proceed to take out student loans for college, then maybe a loan for a new car, and eventually a thirty-year mortgage on a big house we can't afford. Before we know it, we will be so far in debt that we are forced to spend the next twenty-five years working to pay it off.

I remember receiving my first newsletter from Baron Wufot. One of the headlines read, "I Have the Power, the Power of Compounding Interest."

According to the article, if a teen started saving $100 a month at the age of sixteen, with the power of compounding interest, he or she can save over $350,000 by the retirement age of sixty years old. The newsletter showed how to work the math in order to illustrate how powerful compounding interest could be if a person started saving as a teenager.

After reading the article, I thought to myself, I don't know one person worth $350,000. My parents definitely did not have that kind of money. I come from a middle-class family that is happy to have food on the table every night. That day, I set a goal for myself. I would find a job and start saving $100 per month. How hard could it be?

I tried to think of the richest person I know. I couldn't think of anybody who might even have $350,000. It seemed so simple to me. Who couldn't save $100 a month? Eventually, I remembered the richest guy I personally knew was this homeless guy who had just passed away. I would see him in the neighborhood and thought he was some guy without any money or family to watch over him. When he passed away, he had $250,000 sitting in a bank account. Then his daughter materialized out of nowhere, and she gladly claimed the money. Kind of sad, I know. It just goes to show that you can't judge a book by its cover. Other than the homeless man, I don't think I had ever met anyone with $100,000.

Really, how hard could it be to save $100 dollars a month? If I could do that, I would consider myself rich.

At the start, I didn't know the first thing about the stock market. So I read all of Baron Wufot's past newsletters and started spending more time at the library. I checked out every book I could find on the stock market, finance, investing, and economics. I was immediately consumed with reading about the stock market the second I was exposed. The more I read, the more I knew I had to get in the game…like yesterday!

I didn't win the lottery by being born into a rich family. My dad works down on the river docks and my mom is a bank teller. So becoming rich through inheritance was out of the question. I knew that if I was going to become rich, I would have to take the bull by the horns and accomplish it on my own. Just like Baron Wufot.

I learned in Baron Wufot's newsletter that he started investing in the stock market around my age, sixteen. Therefore, I knew there was a way to get in the game. Baron Wufot did it, so can I. The way I look at it is this: I am the only person stopping me from getting a job and finding a way to open my first brokerage savings account.

Other kids aspire to be in a famous rock band or maybe a professional athlete. Who am I to tell them it can't be done? In reality, it has all been done before.

I want to be a stockbroker. My goal this year is to learn how to invest in the stock market and to open my first brokerage (investment) account. I want to start saving $100 a month. Then, one day, I want to study finance in college so I can become a stockbroker on Wall Street.

This is the story of my junior year in high school, which turned out to be the most amazing year of my life. It was the year I opened my first investment account and the year I became a famous investor. Well, kind of!

This is my story...

2

Yoga Team

As I said, I live in St. Louis, Missouri. Or as I like to call it: "Misery." If you are not familiar with where "Misery" is, take your finger and place it right in the middle of a map of the USA. St. Louis, Misery is right smack dab in the middle of the country, and it sits on the banks of the Mississippi River. By the way, I am joking about calling Missouri "Misery." I really do live in a beautiful state. But it's fun to joke about it from time to time.

The first day of school was a hot summer's day. I had just got out for lunch and decided to get some fresh air while I eat my sandwich outside. I was walking around trying to find a shady spot to sit when I spotted some weirdo doing a headstand over by the back of the football field. I decided to investigate who the weirdo was. As I got closer, I realized it was my friend Logi Laru. Duh! Of course, who else could it have been? She's practically the only Indian student at St. Louis High and the only person I know that practices yoga every day. She spends her summers in India with her grandparents, and I hadn't seen her since last year. Oh, and she is practically the most beautiful girl in the solar system.

Logi is the same age as I am, and the only person I know that has the same birthday as me. We were both born on Valentine's Day, February 14th. Logi has short, black hair that she normally wears pulled back. Her short hair silhouettes her face and sets off her emerald green eyes. Her skin tone is a little dusky, close to a natural tan. And probably her most beautiful characteristic is her spirit; she is always smiling and overflowing with kindness. Logi is beautiful. I've pretty much decided we were meant for each other, but I've never had the huevos to confirm it with her.

"What's up, Logi Laru, besides your feet," I asked. God, that was bad. Did I really say that out loud?

"Just doing a little bit of yoga to get me through the day," she said as she fell out of the pose onto her feet. "I find yoga is a great way to clear my mind before physics class. Besides, if you eat a sandwich, then all you want to do is sleep after lunch. Nice move, Mr. 'Biology Sucks!'"

"Very funny, Logi. Not all of us are as rational as you. I guess they don't call you Logical Laru (Logi for short) for nothing," I joked.

Logi is probably the most logical person on the planet. For example, Logi's wardrobe consists of blue jeans and gray shirts. I'm not sure how many pairs of blue jeans and gray shirts she owns. It could be two of each or twenty. They are all the same. She claims that she dresses this way because it is one less decision to make each day and she would like to save her decisions for more important issues than fashion.

Another thing I admire about Logi is that she rides her

bicycle to school every day, just like I do. Huh, I wonder if that has anything to do with us sharing a birthday? You know, because of that horoscope stuff. I never really thought of it until now.

Logi's parents emigrated to the United States for medical school in their twenties. As far as I know, they have lived here ever since. Both of them came from modest Indian families and moved to the States to pursue a better life. They both became successful doctors. I suspect that Logi gets some of her money habits from her parents. I've seen them drop her off on rainy days in a gray, ten-year-old Yotoya Slamry car. They offered to give Logi their old Yotoya Slamry car when she turned sixteen, but of course, she declined their offer. She says that she loves riding her bike so much, she didn't think she would ever own a car.

Unlike Logi, I ride my bicycle to school out of necessity. I live close enough to school that it doesn't make sense for me to take the bus, and far enough away it would take me forever to walk to school. With that said, I actually love the feeling of riding a bicycle. It's great exercise and I love the feeling of flying down the hills. A few years ago, I named my bicycle Disco. My friends think it is hilarious that I name things like my bicycle. It is kind of weird, but the way I look at it is, Disco is a loyal friend of mine so of course he needs a name.

Logi was still working through her weird yoga poses and eventually asked me to join her.

"Come on, Franklin Fi, give it a shot. Yoga is a lot easier than it looks," Logi said.

"Okay, but don't laugh at me when I fall and bust my head. You're the one who is going to have to rush me to the nurse's office," I told her.

Early on in my high school career, I came to the realization that I was never going to run with the cool kids because I don't play sports and I don't drive a nice car. So doing yoga at lunch with Logi definitely wasn't hurting my reputation in the slightest. In fact, it is kind of fun sometimes being a little different. As long as I'm happy and having fun, who cares? What does it matter what other people think of me? There's really not much other kids can say or do to bring me down. I even take some pride in my weirdness.

As we were moving through Logi's yoga routine, it occurred to me that today was the Club Fair, the day students get to choose what club they want to be in for the year. Each student gets to choose one extracurricular club. Last year, I was in the chess club. Chess club was fun, but I definitely knew I didn't want to spend another year playing the same game over and over. Some of the other clubs to choose from are: Future Farmers of America, Debate Team, Car Club, Quilting, Photography, Drama, and Science Club.

"So Logi, what club are you going to sign up for this year?" I asked.

"Definitely not Chess Club again. I didn't feel like I got much out of it," Logi said.

"Yeah, I agree. Chess Club was fun for about the first half of the year. How cool would it be if there was a Stock Market Club?" I commented.

"Concentrate, Franklin. There's no talking in yoga. Turn inward and concentrate on your breathing. Now breathe in and on your out breath, place your left foot back to prepare for Warrior One." Logi continued to instruct me through her yoga routine, but my mind wasn't on yoga. It was on stocks.

After a while, I found myself focusing more on my

breathing and the yoga routine. I had no idea what Warrior One or Two or any of the Warriors were, so I just watched Logi and followed her through the sequence of postures. I was bad, really bad. I couldn't balance on one leg or even touch my toes. Regardless, it actually felt good to do some stretching and to relax.

"You know the average American lives to be eighty?" Logi informed me from the Downward Dog position. "And being sixteen years old, that means we have lived for only one-fifth of our lives. If a person practices yoga throughout their whole life, studies have shown people can extend their average life expectancy to ninety years old."

Logi was pure perspective, she was always saying things that would blow your mind. I had rarely thought about my life past the age of sixteen, and if I did it was to think about college. She got me pondering...then I realized that twenty percent of my life had already passed by and I had not made a single dollar up until this point. Ugh, no more procrastinating! I have to get a job and get in the game!

"What are you chickens doing? Is that what you call Yoda?" came a voice from the distance that could be only one person: Sam Smooth, aka The Royal Smoothness, my best friend. "The force is strong with you tasselled wobbegongs, I can smell it."

Meet Sam "Not So" Smooth. Yes, Smooth is really his last name and yes, that is exactly the opposite of what he is. Like when you call your chubby friend "slim." We call him Smooth because he is clumsy and always saying stupid things. He's always confusing words or tripping over something. What he lacks in gracefulness, he makes up for with his big heart. Smooth would give you the Hawaiian shirt off of his back. Smooth is his name and making you smile is his game.

"Is that pose called the upward frog?" Smooth questioned Logi. "Golly, Franklin, I didn't realize you had gotten all religious on me and took up Yoda."

"Smooth, why don't you quit yapping and join us for a pose or two?" Logi jokingly asked.

"Logi, I haven't seen my feet in years. Do you honestly think I can bend over and touch my toes? If I fall over, you are going to find the football team to help pick me up, okay?" Smooth rambled on.

"Okay, now let's start from the beginning again," Logi said as she restarted her yoga routine. "With your hands at your sides, take a breath in and on your exhale, raise your hands to the sky for mountain pose."

"What do you think I've been doing for the last sixteen years of my life? Pushing air in and out of my lungs for fun?" Smooth joked. "This Yoda is tiring. Is it time for a water break yet?"

"Come on you guys, let's concentrate," Logi pleaded. "Yoga is a chance for you to turn inward and check in with your mind, your body, and your inner self. Now breath in and on your out breath, bend down and touch your toes."

"Well, well, well, if it isn't St. Louis High's very own yoga team," another outside voice interrupted. This time, it was the froggy voice of none other than Malibu Martin.

No, his real name isn't Malibu. We call him Malibu Martin because he never stops talking about all of the cool stuff he does when he visits Malibu, California for the summer. You see, Malibu Martin spends his summers in Malibu with his grandparents. Then we spend the rest of the year hearing about how much better everything is in Malibu.

"Hi, Martin," Logi said, "would you like to join us for a few poses?"

"I would but I forgot my yoga mat at home. Besides, it might mess up my hair. Chicks, chicks, chicks!!! Ah, it's good to be back in school. There are chicks, chicks, chicks everywhere!" Malibu sang as he motioned his hands back and forth like he was spinning vinyls on a turntable.

Martin is what you would call a self-proclaimed pretty boy. He frequents the tanning salon. When he can't make it to the tanning salon, he's not afraid to use fake tanner to keep his orange glow looking fresh. His clothes are always freshly ironed, no matter if he is going to church or third-hour phys ed. I would describe his style as a preppy surfer. If it didn't get too cold in Missouri, he would wear flip-flops and Polo shirts year-round. As for his hair, he has somehow mastered shaping it with gel to make it look like a monster wave in the Pacific Ocean. And yes, the tips of his hair are frosted blond. Today, Malibu Martin was carrying what appeared to be some sort of fanny pack or purse.

"What's in the purse?" Smooth teased.

"It's not a purse, it's a Hucci man bag," Malibu barked at him. "And it really is none of your business what I choose to carry in my man bag."

Smooth and Martin have a brotherly relationship. Both are quick to give the other crap for anything that appears to be a chink in their armor. Though, in the end, Malibu usually gets the best of Smooth. But not today, the man bag was low hanging fruit and Smooth pounced on it like the graceful elephant he is.

"No, really, what kind of stuff do you carry in your purse?" Smooth continued his bombardment. "Let me guess, your purse is where you keep your surfboard wax and hair gel. Catch any killer waves this morning on the Mississippi River?"

Before Malibu could retaliate, Logi interrupted. "Martin, come on and join us for a quick session?"

"Alright, alright, but I don't have my yoga shorts and I have really only practiced Malibu hot yoga before. You are going to have to help a brotha out with his poses," Malibu said.

"No problem! I practice hatha yoga, which I'm guessing Malibu hot yoga is probably derived from. You'll be fine," Logi told him as she began her routine again. "Now, breathe in and on your exhale walk or jump your feet back into Downward Facing Dog. Take three breaths here and then prepare to flow into Upward Facing Dog."

"Logi, where are all these cute dogs that are supposedly facing us?" Smooth questioned.

"You're such an idiot sometimes, Smooth. Those are the names of the yoga poses," Malibu Martin was quick to even the score.

Logi continued as if Smooth and Malibu didn't even exist. After about twenty minutes of yoga, we were all sweating pretty good and the other students were starting to stare. It was my moment to shine, so I started to grunt and breathe louder as I moved through the yoga poses. There is nothing I love more than a few weird looks from a bunch of stiffs. The other students were looking at us like we were Indian snake charmers. It was hilarious. The weird thing about the situation was that we just happened to be in St. Louis, Misery and not in India or at a yoga retreat in Hawaii.

After a while, I lost track of the yoga's meditative spirit and I slipped back into reality. I couldn't stop thinking about how cool it would be if there was a stock market club at our school. The farm kids have their own club, Future Farmers of America. The gearheads have Car Club. Why couldn't there be a Stock Market Club or Personal Finance Club for us to learn about investing in the stock market and making money? It wasn't fair. To me, learning about personal finance seemed like it would be a lot more useful than learning how to play chess or raise a pig. I have nothing against knights and rooks and pigs. They just don't interest me.

Learning to invest in the stock market and making money was all I could think about ever since I started reading Baron Wufot's newsletter. I wanted more than anything in the world to open my own brokerage investment account and to start investing in the stock market. I just had one problem, I didn't have any coin or funds to invest. I had to get a job!

"Do you know why we go to school?" I asked my friends.

"So that we can have the summer off," answered Smooth.

"Good guess, Smooth, but you gotta do better than that," I said.

"To get face time and to pick up girls," Malibu Martin joked. Face time is what Malibu Martin called being seen by all of the hot girls at school. He would hang out in the hallways to say hi to all of the girls as they walked by. It worked for him, but I found it hilarious.

"No, really. Why do you think we go to school?" I asked again.

"Apparently not to do yoga. You guys are the worst at focusing and breathing correctly. We go to school to grow and to learn and to prepare ourselves for college and adulthood," Logi responded.

"They don't call you Logical Laru for nothing!" I told her. "Good answer. Don't you think that is what society wants us to believe? I think we all go to school to learn how to stick to a routine. School is just like work, in that we stick to a schedule. Better be on time or you're in trouble. For the most part, teachers are similar to bosses once we start working. They're always telling us what to do. The uninspiring, boring, overworked teachers we ignore and don't learn anything from them. The only teachers I listen and pay attention to are the fun teachers that I respect. These are the teachers that make going to school worthwhile. They understand that by making learning fun, we may actually retain something that will last for the rest of our lives. I have a feeling the work environment is the same way. The way I see it, we are just being herded through a system. We're not learning anything that millions of other kids before us haven't learned. We're just doing what society and the system expect from us. It's all one big formula. First, we go to school to learn discipline. Then onto college, where you figure out what field you want to work in. While you are there, you pick up some debt from student loans. Once you have figured out what industry you want to work in, you're ready to enter the workforce to pay off the $40,000 you owe in student loans. Once you start making money and have become comfortable with paying off student loan debt, you decide to take out another loan for a car. Before you know it, you are married with kids and have decided to take out an even bigger loan. This time, borrowing hundreds of thousands of dollars for a thirty-year mortgage on a house. A house that you will then spend the rest of your lives trying to pay off so one day you can retire when you're too old to walk and can barely use the bathroom on your own."

"My goodness, Franklin, you are not allowed to do any more Yoda for the rest of your life. Or are you back on Baron Wufot's magic potion again? What has gotten into you?" Smooth asked.

"The system has developed this formula for us to follow, Smooth," I continued. "And I am not going down that path for the next forty years. I have been thinking a lot about it and I want to break free from the formula. I want to live my life and respect the system, but use it to my advantage. I want to be able to make money on my own and not depend on some degree that says I'm smart. All I have been able to think about lately is the stock market, making money, and Baron Wufot's newsletter. You see, my plan is to go to school and learn how the system works, so I can use it to my advantage. I don't plan on letting the system take advantage of this hombre. I'll learn how to beat the system. Then I won't be stuck paying off debt for the rest of my life. Plus, I want to learn the stuff that I find interesting. I want to see the world!"

"Franklin Fi, what in all of the houses of the holy does this have to do with Yoda and the Upward Frog?" Smooth commented.

"It's called the Upward Dog, not the Upward Frog," Logi corrected him. "And I think you dogs have the attention spans of toddlers."

"That's what I said, I said frog. Sheesh!" Smooth said in disbelief.

"I'm trying to explain that I want to learn about the stock market now, like yesterday. In order to do that, I propose that we start a stock market club. If we can learn to invest, then we can forge our own path and break free of the formula that leads to a lifetime of debt," I told them.

"Boom shaka-laka! Franklin Fi, you are a freaking maniac! I like the way you think, but you think the teachers are going to let us start a new club on the day of the club fair?" Malibu Martin croaked in his froggy voice.

"Why don't we ask Mr. Crutchfield to sponsor us? He is always talking about how we have to learn to think on our own. I bet he is going to love this idea!" I told the yoga team.

"I'm in like the Flintstones! Count me in," Smooth quipped.

"Smooth, I think you meant to say that you are 'in like Flynn,' as in Errol Flynn," Logi corrected him again.

"Sheesh! Logi, do you hear the words coming out of my mouth? That's what I said."

"Ribbit, count me in. I will do anything to get out of St. Louis, Misery. This city ain't big enough for Malibu Martin. *Malibu*, now that's my city, baby!" Malibu Martin agreed.

"I still think we should start a Yoga Club, but I can see you guys have your mind set on the Stock Market Club. So count me in…like Wilma, Wilma Flintstone," joked Logi, "but on one condition. If this works, you all have to promise me you'll continue to do yoga with me at lunch," Logi said.

"Gladly!" I said. "We've got ten minutes left of lunchtime, let's go find Mr. Crutchfield and ask him if he will sponsor our Stock Market Club. There he is, over by the gym door. Let's go!"

3

Stock Market Club

"**C**an you believe that Professor Crutchfield thought our idea was brilliant? He actually said brilliant!" I exclaimed. "He even agreed to sponsor our club and talk to the other teachers to get their approval."

The seventh hour was upon us and we were at the club fair. This was our chance to showcase the Stock Market Club and recruit fellow classmates into the club. Unfortunately, being that we had just come up with the idea a couple of hours earlier, it didn't go very well. All we had was a dirty old table and a piece of paper that said "$tock Market Club" on it, handwritten in Sharpie.

We added exactly zero new club members that glorious day. Apparently, all of the other students had already made up their minds beforehand. It was a little embarrassing, but I was so excited that I really didn't care. Professor Crutchfield reassured us it was okay that no one else joined our club. In fact, it was probably a good thing. We could use this school year to develop the format of the club and to try different things to see what worked and what didn't. He made a good point: we really knew nothing about the stock market or even how to discuss it.

Our First Meeting

"Okay, now that we are the owners of a brand new Stock Market Club, what shall we discuss?" Smooth asked.

"Believe it or not, St. Louis is not the first high school to have a Stock Market Club," Professor Crutchfield informed us. "There are actually many Stock Market Clubs throughout the country and I wouldn't be surprised if there wasn't another club in Misery. Oops, I meant Missouri."

"How about we study a different stock or company each week?" Logi suggested.

"That's not a bad idea," I said. "We could even take it a step further and study a different sector each month. That way, we would be studying multiple companies within the same sector each month."

"Slow your pigs," joked Smooth. "What's all this talk about scepters? Are you talking about one of the infinity stones in the scepter that Loki used to carry with him in one of those superhero movies?"

"Yeah, something like that, your Smoothness," I told him. "A sector is a group of companies in the same industry that investors have grouped together to be able to analyze them better. I think there are ten or eleven sectors. For example, here are some of the sectors I can think of off the top of my head: energy, financials, technology, telecom, and healthcare."

"Slow down, Franklin," Malibu Martin interrupted with a

croak. "I thought this was going to be fun and we were going to make some Benjamins in the process. You know, some coin, some funds, some shillings, some paper, some scratch."

"Okay, we get the point. You're right. We need to make this club fun and learn about the stock market. What do you suggest?" I asked him.

"We could start a fantasy stock market league. Like a fantasy football league, but with stocks instead of players," Malibu Martin suggested.

"That's stupid," barked Smooth. "We could hold a draft of companies and only get so many trades a week or a month. We could even have a draft night and I'll bring the carrot sticks!"

"Guys, for once I think your bickering has led to something brilliant. This is the greatest idea in the history of the universe!" I yelled. "We could start with $10,000 in virtual money and hold a draft before week one kicks off. Then each month, we are only allowed to make a maximum of ten trades, as in, 'buy or sell' ten stocks."

"I'm really good with spreadsheets. I could track the trades and money from week to week," Logi added.

"This is seriously the best idea ever!" I shouted in excitement. "We should write Baron Wufot to tell him about our idea. He gives away two or three scholarships each year to high school students, maybe he'll even sponsor our competition. We could ask him to put up a small amount, like a hundred dollars or something. That way, the winner can open their very own brokerage savings account."

"Yeah! Good idea, Franklin. A hundred bucks, that's popcorn to Baron Wufot!" Smooth added.

"Peanuts, that's peanuts, Smooth. Not popcorn," Malibu Martin corrected him.

Smooth would not be discouraged. "Just think, if I could win the competition, I would be the star of St. Louis High School. I might even be the first student in the galaxy to win a prize for anthropology."

We all made a pact to correct Smooth no more than once in a five-minute period, so we let his statement about anthropology slide because none of us were sure what he meant.

"It can't hurt to write him a letter. At the very least, he'll be excited to hear we've been reading his newsletter and that he inspired us to start a Stock Market Club. I'll even write the letter," I told the rest of the club.

4

The Richest Man in the Solar System

"Tater, can you please bring me another Diet Dr. Pep?" Baron Wufot shouted across the office at his personal assistant. He refused to use a telephone to call someone in the same office. Back when Baron Wufot got into the business, that's how you got things done and it hasn't changed since. He refuses to use a phone or computer to ask for something from his personal assistant.

Tater Higgins is Baron Wufot's personal assistant and has worked for him ever since he founded the company sixty-plus years ago. They are quite the duo. Baron Wufot drinks Diet Dr. Pep, and Tater Higgins drinks rooibos ginger tea. Baron Wufot enjoys a burger for lunch, and Tater prefers a kale salad. Tater is a practicing vegan, and Baron Wufot is a practicing burger monster. I think you get the idea.

"Here's your Diet Dr. Pep, sir, and the celery sticks you

asked for. That's your fourth Diet Dr. Pep this morning and last one for the day, under my watch at least. You know I told your wife I would limit you to four a day," Tater told him.

"Tater, she doesn't have to know. How long have we been friends? Plus, you've got me choking down all of these veggies. You know good and well that I didn't ask for celery sticks. But I would rather eat them than hear you complain about my diet. Doesn't that count for something?" Baron begged.

"Yap, that means I am the only person on Wall Street that has leverage on the famous Baron Wufot," joked Tater.

"Haha-haha-haha! Tater, what would I do without you? You're a riot!" Baron gave a big belly laugh.

"Oh, sir, you just got this in the mail. It appears to be more fan mail from one of your teen followers. The letter is from a Franklin Fi, and the return address is St. Louis High School. Would you like me to open it for you?" Tater said as he presented Baron with the letter.

"Great, I love getting mail from the kiddos. It means they have been reading my newsletter," Baron said as he snatched the letter from Tater and ripped it open with his teeth.

Dear Mr. Wufot,

My name is Franklin Fi, and I am a junior at St. Louis High School in St. Louis, Missouri. I started reading your newsletter last year. It's fantastic! I think I have read each newsletter at least five times. Please hurry up and write more of them. If you can't tell, you've totally got me hooked on learning about the stock market. All I can think about is being a stockbroker when I grow up.

My classmates and I have started the first ever Stock Market Club at our high school. Because it is a new club at our school, we are swimming in uncharted waters and developing the club as we go along.

At our last meeting, we came up with the idea to start a "fantasy stock market league." It is going to be similar to a fantasy football league but instead with stocks. For example, we plan on holding a draft night for stocks, instead of football players. Each participant will begin with $10,000 in virtual money. Once the competition begins, participants will be allowed to make ten trades a month. The competition will last six months.

The reason I am writing to you today is to ask you to sponsor the competition. We are seeking a sponsor to help us fund a brokerage account that will be rewarded to the winner of the competition. We're not looking for a large donation, maybe a hundred dollars. Just enough to get the rest of the club members excited about the stock market.

I realize this is a lot to ask. We are all big fans of your newsletter and we will continue to follow it regardless. The newsletter has been a big inspiration in my life this past year. Every month, I eagerly await the release of the next newsletter. It's the highlight of my month.

Thank you for taking time out of your busy schedule to read this letter. Any correspondence is greatly appreciated.

Sincerely,
Franklin Fi

"Oh, hot damn!" Baron Wufot yelled as he jumped out of his seat. "Tater, I love getting letters like this from the kiddos. It makes me realize that I am not wasting my time writing that monthly newsletter. Can you check into how I can donate this money and make sure that it is all legal?"

"Of course, sir, I will get right on it," Tater replied.

5

High School Stock Market Competition

Dear Franklin,

It would be an honor to sponsor your fantasy stock market competition. It is the most amazing idea ever! Thank you for reaching out to me. If I am to sponsor the competition, I would like to request a couple of changes to the regulations.

1. The competition will be open to all high school students in the United States.

2. After you have initially "drafted" or chosen your stocks, I ask that you are only able to make two trades per month, instead of ten trades a month. Trading that many stocks in such a short amount of time is a horrible habit for any investor. I don't want to teach teens any bad habits. Also, I want to limit the participants to two trades a month in order to force

them to put more thought into each trade. Having patience and making calculated decisions are a very important part of investing, and I want to ensure you kiddos learn this from the start.

I will have my tech team develop a platform for the competition that will track the standings and monetary value for each participant's portfolio. If you are willing, I would like for you to help my tech team with the development of the app. I want to make sure we fulfill your vision.

Also, I have decided to award the winner with a $10,000 brokerage savings account, not the $100 that you initially asked for. The only stipulation on the account is that the winner will not be able to withdraw any money from the account for the first ten years. I want the winner to learn the value of compounding interest and I believe this is the best way to demonstrate it.

Fantastic idea, kiddo, and thank you for reaching out to me.

Kindest regards,
Baron Wufot

P.S. My personal assistant, Tater Higgins, will be contacting you in the near future. He will put you in touch with the head of my tech team so that you can help with the development of the stock market competition app.

6

A Beginner's Investment Strategy

The stock market competition was official. Not only had we started a Stock Market Club at our high school, but now we were also responsible for launching a nationwide, high school stock market competition. The idea was a stroke of genius on the part of Malibu Martin and Smooth. The backing of Baron Wufot, the richest man in the solar system, made it official and now there was a chance of it becoming an annual event.

A month passed and I worked out the kinks with Tater, Baron's assistant. His team developed the cell phone app, and I provided input from the student perspective. It was a really cool experience getting to see how a cell phone app was developed from beginning to end. The best part, I finally had some real-life work experience. You'd better believe it is going on that blank sheet of paper I call my resume. I'm probably the only kid in the world that can claim that I collaborated with Baron Wufot on a tech project.

The competition was set to be announced in Baron Wufot's October newsletter. The competition would begin on October 15th. Those two weeks would give the participants time to prepare for the first-ever high school stock market competition.

"Have you all seen the latest Baron Wufot newsletter?" I exclaimed as I walked into the Stock Market Club meeting. "Things just got real. I'll read it to you!"

Baron Wufot'$
Personal Finance Newsletter for Teens
October 1

$10,000 High School Stock Market Competition—First Annual

Rules and Regulations:

- » Open to all current high school students in the United States of America

- » Each student will manage a $10,000 virtual portfolio of stocks

- » Stock selections must be submitted by October 15th

- » The competition runs six months and ends on April 15th
- » Each participant will have a maximum of two trades per month
- » Standings will be released on the first business day of each month
- » The winner will be announced on April 15th at the close of the stock market
- » The winner will receive a brokerage account funded with $10,000 of real money. The money in the account cannot be withdrawn for a period of ten years.

A special thanks to the St. Louis High School's Stock Market Club for proposing the competition.

This has been a Baron Wufot Production. Remember, kiddos, pick 'em to hold 'em and let compound interest do the rest.

Your friend,
Baron Wufot

"This is so exciting, Franklin!" Logi said.

"Don't thank me. This was all Smooth's and Malibu's idea. If they weren't such good friends and didn't enjoy debating, we may never have come up with the idea," I joked.

"It was my idea," Malibu Martin claimed.

"Whatever, dude, I'm not going to let you steal my rainbow! You know it was my idea," Smoothilicious retorted.

"That's *thunder* and I'm not trying to steal your pot of gold…leprechaun boy," Malibu snapped back.

I thought about letting them argue a bit longer with the hope that we might get another brilliant idea out of them. But I could see this argument was going nowhere, so I interrupted them.

"We have both of you to thank for coming up with the idea of the stock market competition," I praised. "Once we raise some funds for the Stock Market Club, I will see that a statue is erected or a plaque made commemorating the day that you two clowns came up with the idea of the competition."

"That would be awesome. If you have a statue made, make sure to shave some LBs (pounds) off my belly. As for Malibu's statue, you should make him even shorter than he already is and enlarge that big frog mouth of his," Smooth requested.

"Alright, enough joking around. We've only got an hour for the club. Let's get started," I told them.

"Okey dokey, boss. Where do we start?" Malibu asked.

Since it was our first club meeting and we had failed to make any agenda whatsoever, I was at a loss of ideas. Then, right on time as usual, Logi chimed in to save the day.

"Why don't we take five minutes to meditate? It will clear our minds and I'm sure the path will reveal itself," Logi suggested.

"That is a great idea, but Logi, you will have to lead us. I don't think anybody else here knows how to meditate," I told her. This also gave me a few minutes to collect myself and come up with an agenda.

"Speak for yourself. I spent the summer meditating at the temple in Malibu," Malibu Martin claimed.

"Sure you did. All of this cool stuff always happens to you

in Malibu, but I have yet to see proof of any of it," Smooth prodded him.

"You guys need to find a peaceful place in your heart for each other. Now, let's get started!" Logi began. "Start by getting into the Lotus position or as some of you might call it, 'criss-cross applesauce' seated position. We are going to start with an exercise called box breathing.

With your eyes closed, breathe in through your nose while counting to three.

1-2-3

Now hold your breath and count to three again.

1-2-3

Slowly exhale while counting to three.

1-2-3

With all of the air out of your body count to three again.

1-2-3

Now, we are going to repeat this process.

Inhale 1-2-3

Hold 1-2-3

Exhale 1-2-3

Hold 1-2-3

Now, repeat this process on your own and concentrate on your breath and nothing else."

We repeated the process for what seemed like years. I was half afraid that we were going to come out of the meditation and the stock market challenge was already going to be over.

Ding!!!

The digital bell on Logi's meditation app went off. It was amazing, I felt energized and more clear-headed. It was as if I had taken a thirty-minute siesta.

"Now, let's continue," I said to the group. "Any ideas?"

"Why don't you go around the room and discuss what kinds of stocks we plan to invest in for the stock market competition," Professor Crutchfield suggested from the back of the classroom where he was grading papers.

"I hardly know what the stock market is. Can someone give me a quick definition of the stock market?" Smooth asked.

"Sure thing, Smooth," Logi started to answer. "Just think of the stock market like it was any other market. For example, say you go to the flower market and you want to buy some roses for your mom. Each one of the vendors will offer a slightly different price for their roses. If it is around Valentine's Day, the price of roses will go up due to the high demand. The stock market is the same concept. It is a market where investors go to buy shares (partial ownership) in companies. Another name for a share is a stock. Therefore, it is called the stock market. If there is a high demand for a company, then the stock price of that company will go up. Just like roses around Valentine's Day!"

"Wow, I think I kind of understand what you are talking about," Smooth stated.

"Now that we know what the stock market is all about, I think it is a fantastic idea that we go around the room and discuss what stocks we might like to purchase, as Professor Crutchfield suggested. Then, we could go around the room and discuss our investment styles for the competition," I said.

"Franklin Fi, you have drunk way too much of Baron Wufot's magic potion," Malibu Martin joked. "Do you honestly think any of us have an investment style? Last I checked, we're just a bunch of broke sixteen-year-olds who have never made a trade in our lives."

"That's not true, Malibu Martin. You have an investment style. You think the more you invest in your style, the more chicks will dig you. Exhibit A, the man purse," Smooth ripped Malibu Martin again.

"Smooth, I don't know why you keep ripping on Malibu Martin's man purse. I think it would look great with your combo of Hawaiian shirt, cargo shorts, and aqua shoes," Logi told him.

Smooth truly is a force to be reckoned with. He stands over six feet tall and is just about as round as he is high. Throw a Hawaiian shirt on him and he is a walking tropical forest. To top it all off, Smooth has blond, curly hair that he wears puffed out kind of like an afro. Based on his appearance, I think it is safe to say that Smooth is more likely to fit in at a county fair than at Muscle Beach.

"You guys need to relax. Remember this is supposed to be fun. I will walk you through the process," I said. "Smooth, let's start with you. Start by naming five companies that you like or support by purchasing their products."

"I can do that. Is it really that easy?" Smooth asked.

"No, but work with me, Mr. Smootherific," I begged.

"Here it goes," Smooth began…

1. My first company is PearMob. I own a PearPhone, a PearWatch, and a PearTab. I love all of them, so why not buy some stock in PearMob. That's my number one choice!

2. Yotoya Cars is my second choice. If I could have any car in the universe, it would be a Yotoya 4racer. Plus, Momma Smooth has a Yotoya Slamry with 300,000 miles on it and she's had zero problems. So Yotoya Cars is my second pick.

3. Pichotle Mexican is my next pick. I could have owned the whole company by now if I was only buying stock in Pichotle instead of burritos. I practically eat there every day. Pichotle is my third pick.

4. For my next company, how about Hikee Shoes. It is the only brand of shoes this bad baller wears. Even to church. I wear my all-black Hikee Chokes to church every Sunday. Then they go back in the box. I talked Papa Smooth into spending $350 on those bad boys.

5. Lastly, how about Litup Studios. I'm not just picking Litup Studios because of their blockbuster movies. Did you know they own the franchises of Star Messiah, the Marbella comic book movies, along with the One-Eyed Red Monster Movies, plus they have all of those old-school, hand-drawn movies like *The Prince Sorcerer*. Yeah, Litup Studios is definitely a top five pick for me.

"Boom-shaka-laka!" I yelled. "Smooth, you are a freaking maniac. Those are all solid companies. Eventually, you'll need to look into their financials. But all of that stuff can wait.

I think you have five solid companies to start with. As the competition starts, you can learn more about these companies and decide if you want to hold onto them or you may even decide to sell them and buy shares in other companies.

"Wow, it's that easy!" Smooth said as he smiled from ear to ear while doing a little jig and singing, "I'm going to win $10,000. I'm going to win $10,000. I'm going to win $10,000."

"I wish it was that easy. Though I think you chose some good companies and you have a good base to learn from," I complimented him.

"Okay, who's next?" I asked.

"If Smooth can do it, so can I," Malibu Martin volunteered. "Being a California boy, I'm going to go with all technology stocks."

Malibu Martin was born in Malibu, California but moved to St. Louis, Missouri when he was one year old. Nonetheless, he's always referred to himself as a California boy.

"Let's hear it, Bu-Baby," Logi cheered on Malibu Martin.

"Here are my top five tech stocks:

1. Biloogle Inc.

2. Slividia Semiconductors

3. Petjix Entertainment

4. PearMob

5. Basebook Ai

Tech's been hot and I think this will give me the best chance of winning in the six-month time period of the competition. That's a short investment window, so you got to go big or go home. Boom-shaka-laka-shaka-laka. You all know I got this!" Malibu shouted as he beat his chest with his fist.

"Alright, now we're rolling. Malibu, you have a good point. It is a super short time period to be investing. I like your thought process," I told him. "Remember, we still have a couple of weeks to go until the competition kicks off. Don't feel like you have to just invest in five stocks. That was just an easy number for Smooth to start with."

Typically, investing your whole portfolio in one sector is kind of risky. It is definitely not something I would suggest, but it might work in his favor in this situation. Malibu could get lucky with technology stocks and they could make a big move up over the next six months. The opposite could happen as well, technology stocks tend to move fast in whatever direction they are headed. They could just as easily take a dive to the downside. The smarter move would be to diversify a little bit and add some stocks from different sectors to your portfolio. The reality of the matter was that none of us really knew what we were doing and this would be a great opportunity to learn a bit more about the market.

"Alright, you're up, Princess Logi," I said with a smile.

"I think it is best if I stick to what I know," Logi began. "For beginners, I am going to start by investing half of my portfolio in an S&P 500 Index Fund. Historically, this type of fund has annually returned 7% or better. Being that this is a six-month competition, I feel fairly certain that it will return 3% or better. If for some reason the market as a whole is down, I feel that this index fund will be a good defensive play. Overall, my approach is going to be to play it conservatively and to use this competition as a way to work on my real life investment strategy."

"Ummm, would you like to tell us rookies what an index fund is?" Malibu Martin asked.

"Sure thing!" Logi said. "An index fund is a type of a mutual fund or Exchange Traded Fund (ETF) that reflects the index it is tracking. Basically, if you buy an index fund that reflects the S&P 500 Index, as the S&P 500 Index goes up 2%, so will your index fund that is designed to mirror it. It is a way of owning all of the stocks in the index without having to buy all 500 stocks. A mutual fund buys them all for you and then offers them to their investors as a single product. Of course, many mutual funds will charge a fee for providing the product. So you have to make sure the management fee isn't too high before you buy the mutual fund. Does that clear things up for you?"

"Yeah, kind of. So basically you are buying the whole stock market, which is a way of diversifying your portfolio. And this index fund is the easiest way for you to buy the whole market without having to make a million trades," Malibu brilliantly summarized. It seemed like he knew more about the market than he originally let on.

"Confusing and complicated, but I guess that is what I signed up for by being alive," Smooth told us as he ran his hands through his long, blond curly hair.

"Smooth, any time I see or hear a term that I don't understand, I just look it up online. There are a ton of websites out there that define financial terms for you," I added.

"I can see where you are coming from," Logi continued, "but believe it or not, index funds are actually supposed to simplify things and are known as a low-cost, conservative investment. Don't get frustrated, the more I learn about the stock market, the more I realize how little I know about it."

"Thanks, Logi, that makes me feel like I'm the first fish that tried to walk after slithering out of the ocean. What do they say, you've got to dance before you can crawl? Well, I'm just over here trying to squirm my way to your level," joked Smooth.

"Smooth, you really shouldn't get frustrated," Logi comforted him. "Little by little. You have the rest of your life to figure this stuff out, so don't get down on yourself. Investing in an index fund is my way of making the logical investment. I don't know a lot about the market, so I'm trying to keep it simple."

"And that is why they call you Logical Laru," I told her. She's definitely not your typical, irrational teenager. I like to think Logi and I are similar in the sense that we both enjoy the thought process of making a conscious decision. Or maybe, this trait is what is holding me back sometimes? For example, I have always wanted to ask Logi on a date, but the rational side of me says I shouldn't risk ruining a friendship. The other side of my brain is telling me that one of these days I've got to get up the nerve to ask her on a date, maybe even to prom.

"So, what are you going to do with the other 50% of your money?" Smooth inquired.

"Okay, now that I have made the S&P 500 index fund the backbone of my portfolio, I am going to invest the other half in stocks that stand to benefit from upcoming short-term trends," Logi began to explain. "It will be comprised of the following:

1. Holly Inc., because Christmas is coming up and every girl wants diamond-encrusted jewelry for Christmas.

Diamonds are controlled by only a few companies and Holly Inc. can demand whatever prices they want. Some would say they have a monopoly on diamonds.

2. Litup Studios is my next choice and, yes, I agree with Smoothilicious on this one. Plus, it is another play on the holiday season. Litup Studios always releases their best movies during the holiday season. They have a new edition to the Star Messiah series called *Children of Alpha*. Plus, they have another animated movie from their Scooters franchise. It's called *Scooters Reloaded*, and it comes out in time for the holidays. Both are projected to be the top-grossing movies of the holiday season.

3. Balookaa.com Inc. Yes, once again, this is another play on Christmas. Balookaa is the largest online retailer. Their stock price has been going straight up for years, and I think it will continue to go up for at least six more months. Practically everyone does their Christmas shopping online these days. I think Balookaa will be the star of my virtual portfolio.

For now, that is going to round out my portfolio."

"Bravo, bravo!" I chanted. "It didn't even occur to me to factor in the holidays. I like your style, Logi Laru. You logically sized up the competition by taking the time period of the contest into account and then considering what seasonal trends your portfolio could benefit from. Good work!"

"Stop it," Logi said as she blushed. "My selections are very conservative and I'm sure I'll end up somewhere in the middle of the pack. There's no way this portfolio will win. I just can't bring myself to gamble on some unproven stocks. And I'm okay with that. I told myself I wanted to use this competition to learn more about the market and to see if this is a strategy I might use with my portfolio in the future."

"Which leaves the man with all the answers, Baron's disciple, the Stan Musial of the stock market. Mr. Boombastic, his stocks are very fantastic. The one. The only... Franklin Fi. You're up dude!" Smooth said in his best announcer voice.

"Yeah, let's hear it, Franklin. We've all gone, it's your turn, boss," Malibu Martin croaked in his froggy voice.

Franklin's Investment Style

"Come on, you guys. Everything I know about the stock market I've learned in the last six months from Baron Wufot's newsletter and the finance books I have read from the library. I hope you guys don't think I am a know-it-all, I am just trying to give you all a fighting chance in this competition," I told them.

"Gosh, Franklin. We're just giving you a hard time," Smooth added. "I wouldn't even be interested in the stock market if it wasn't for you. Before you started talking about the stock market, I just thought it was something old people complained about. Stuff like, 'we're never going to be able to retire now that our mutual fund is worth half of what it was last year' and 'honey, you better sell our mutual fund before it drops another 50%!' That was always the talk around the Smooth household. Little did I know, my parents were making the not-so-smooth decisions by investing in expensive mutual funds and selling them at the bottom. Franklin, I am glad you have taught me a thing or two about the stock market. One of these days, I am going to get some money and start investing. First things first though, this hombre needs to get a jobby job."

"Smooth, have you been drinking Baron Wufot's magic potion today?" Logi joked.

"Okay, boss diesel, what do you got? Let's hear it!" Malibu croaked at me.

Franklin began, "Alright, for starters, you all have some awesome stock ideas. Some ideas I might have to borrow. It's actually very possible I will use some of those ideas in my portfolio. First, I plan to come up with a list of ten to twenty stocks that I'll call my watchlist. Over the next two weeks, I'll evaluate these stocks and figure out which ones offer the most growth potential while being the most attractive to buy at the best value. Just because a stock is growing rapidly doesn't mean the stock is a good value. Stocks can be overpriced just like a car or a purse. For example, Malibu, what if you bought or invested in a Hucci man bag two years ago when it cost half as much?"

"Rad, I probably would have bought two of those man bags and sold the other one for a profit a couple of years later," Malibu Martin commented.

"That's exactly right! My point is that once everybody decides something is cool, then economic demand takes over and drives up the price. Stocks are the same, you want to be the investor who finds growth companies before they become popular and overbought," I continued with another example. "Smooth, take your shoes for example, those first-edition Hikee Chokes. When they first hit the market back in the mid-1980s, they cost $60 to $70 for a pair. Now how much do they cost? Last I checked, they were going north of $300. Just imagine if you could have bought a few pairs back in the 1980s and then sold them twenty years later. That's around a 400% profit. I'm not saying that Hikee Chokes aren't worth $300. They are because that is the price consumers are willing to pay for them. Would you rather be the consumer who bought a pair for $70 or the consumer who paid $300? That's a 400% profit versus a 0% profit. Stocks are the same way! The first step is finding a pair of first-edition Hikee Chokes before anyone else does. The second step is being confident enough in your investment approach to know you are buying an undervalued product or stock that will most definitely increase in value over some given amount of time. This type of investing is what Baron Wufot calls 'value investing,' Because you are buying financially sound companies that are trading at a discounted value. It all goes back to buy low and sell high."

"If it is so easy, then why aren't all of us spic-and-span rich?" Smooth asked.

"That's 'filthy rich,' not 'spic-and-span rich.' Where do you come up with this stuff, your Royal Smoothness?" Malibu corrected him.

"For starters, it is more difficult than it sounds or we would all be spic-and-span rich! Furthermore, we don't have a coin to invest, which is a wee bit of a problem," I told them. "The real challenge is to decide at what price a stock is cheap and then having the patience to wait for it to drop to that level. So says Baron Wufot. Or in the case of your first-edition Hikee Chokes, you would have needed to anticipate they were going to quadruple in price over the next twenty years and bought as many pairs as possible."

"I wasn't even a twinkle in momma Smooth's eye in 1985,

so no, I could not have guessed. But I see your point. This stock investing stuff is kind of like seeing the future," Smooth stated.

"So, I guess I'm saying that I am going to choose my favorite twenty or so stocks. Then evaluate them to figure which of them may be undervalued and could possibly sell at a higher price in the next six months, which is the length of the competition. Like Logi, I want to use this competition to try out my investment strategy. If I get lucky and win, then of course, I would be over the moon. But if I lose, I at least want to walk away having learned something about investing in the stock market," I told the group.

"Dude, you really take this stuff serendipitously!" exclaimed Smooth.

"Seriously, Smooth. I think you meant to say 'seriously,' not 'serendipitously.' You are something else, my friend," Malibu Martin said.

"Good point, Franklin. Baron gave us fourteen days for a reason. We've all got some work to do," added Logi. "How do you propose we evaluate companies, or how would Baron Wufot do it?"

"To begin with, I am going to spend a couple of days going over Baron Wufot's newsletters from last year. I'm far from an expert on the topic," I continued. "While reviewing the newsletters, I am going to take notes and try to pinpoint what metrics Baron Wufot uses to evaluate stocks. For example, I know that Baron likes low P/E stocks and companies with high-profit margins."

"Okay, you lost me at P/E. Are we playing basketball again today in P.E.?" Smooth asked. He had obviously not been listening.

"That's P backslash E, as in the P/E ratio. It stands for the Price to Earnings Ratio. The Price to Earnings Ratio is a simple metric used by investors to determine if the stock is over or underpriced. You can find it by dividing the company's **P**rice per share by **E**arnings per share. Baron talks about it in his newsletter all of the time," I explained.

"Why don't we make that homework for the next meeting," Logi added. We could find and use the Baron Wufot newsletter as a guide or a blueprint for our meetings. For homework, let's all define what the P/E ratio is and then list the P/E ratio for each of the companies that we decide to invest in. It will be a great learning experience."

"Homework! I thought this club was going to be fun? Besides, I don't even do my homework in my other classes," Malibu Martin said in his froggy voice.

"Come on, you all. How are we ever going to learn about the stock market and investing if we don't put any work into this. This will seriously take five minutes to do. The alternative is we can continue to be lazy and spend the next twenty years floundering in debt trying to figure out what happened with our lives and why we don't have any money. Then, after you have racked up student loan debt, credit card debt, and debt on your house, you might just decide you'd better learn something about saving and investing. By that time, you are going to be old and fat and unmotivated to do anything but watch the St. Louis Cardinals' baseball games on TV. That's not going to happen on my watch. I promise this club will be a lot more worthwhile than any class you're taking at STL High. Let's forge a new path for our lives. It will 'serendipitously' take five minutes," I preached.

"Sounds delightening, count me in," Smooth commented

as he made a note to look up the physical education ratios for his companies.

"I think you meant to say 'enlightening,' not 'delightening,'" Logi corrected him. "And P/E stands for Price to Earnings Ratio, not physical education."

"Sheesh, that's what I said. You all need to clean your ears out every once in a while," Smooth said.

"Alright, count me in. You made a good point about this stuff being useful later on in life. Is that really what people do? Why would anybody think it was a good idea to accumulate all of that debt? My plan is to be rich and live in Malibu. And that doesn't come easy. You know, you can't buy a home for less than ten million dollars in Malibu," Malibu Martin informed us.

"Alright, all of you, we are about out of time. Does anybody else have anything to add before the bell rings?" I asked.

"Nope," they all said at once.

"Okay, I think we will adjourn our first meeting. Have a good weekend, if I don't see you," I said as I started putting away my notebook.

"Oh, that reminds me," Logi cut in. "Does anybody want to go to the City Museum this weekend with me? On Saturday night, it's teen night from nine to eleven."

"That sounds awesome! The City Museum is practically the coolest place on the planet," I answered.

"That place is for kids. Besides, I got tickets to the Justin Sleeper concert. He just came out with a new album. Have you heard his new jam, 'Coffee Ground Daydream'? It's lit, as in cool, as in poppin'! Plus, there are going to be so many chicks there. Chicks! Chicks! Chicks!" Malibu Martin said as he was dancing around.

"Dude, stop. You know I love Justin Sleeper. How did you get tickets to his concert?" I asked.

"I stayed up all night waiting in line at the ticket office. It was stupid cold, but I got 'em!" Malibu Martin informed us.

"What about you, Smooth, you in?" I asked.

"Nah, um, sorry, I can't go. I have to go to my cousin's bar mitzvah," Smooth responded.

"What are you talking about. You're not even Jewish," I said.

"Yeah, but my aunt married a Jewish guy and we get invited to all of their cool celebrations," Smooth told us.

"Looks like it is just you two lovebirds for Saturday night. It's about time you two go on a date," Malibu Martin teased us.

I turned bright red and then...

Brrrrriiiiinnnngggggg!!! Brrrrriiiiinnnngggggg!!! Brrrrriiiiinnnngggggg!!!

"Saved by the bell," Smooth said with a laugh.

7

How to Get Your First Job

That Friday after school, I started to make a list of all the places I could possibly get a job. Then, I recalled that Baron Wufot had actually written about this in one of his newsletters. Maybe it was the June edition or another one of those just before summer break. If I recall correctly, it was one of the newsletters Baron was discussing the power of compounding interest, which doesn't help me much because it seems like he mentions compound interest in almost every one of his newsletters.

After digging for a while, I finally found the newsletter I was looking for:

Baron Wufot'$
Personal Finance Newsletter for Teens
June 1

Compounding Interest: How to turn $100 a month into $450,000 at retirement.

If you contribute $100 per month ($1,200 each year) into a brokerage investment account until retirement, then it is possible to have over $450,000 at the retirement age of 64 years old. That is assuming the stock market's historical average rate of return is 7% per year. **Kiddos, that is the power of compounding interest!**

How to turn $100 a month into $450,000 at retirement

Starting Value = $0.00

Contribution = $100 per month (equals $1,200 per year)

Historical Market Average Return = 7%

Years = 48 years

Age	Balance	Age	Balance
16	$0.00	41	$81,211.76
17	$1,284.00	42	$88,180.59
18	$2,657.88	43	$95,637.23
19	$4,127.93	44	$103,615.84
20	**$5,700.89**	45	$112,152.94
21	$7,383.95	46	$121,287.65
22	$9,184.83	47	$131,061.79
23	$11,111.76	48	$141,520.11
24	$13,173.59	49	$152,710.52
25	$15,379.74	**50**	**$164,684.25**
26	$17,740.32	51	$177,496.15
27	$20,266.14	52	$191,204.88
28	$22,968.77	53	$205,873.22
29	$25,860.59	54	$221,568.35
30	**$28,954.83**	55	$238,362.13
31	$32,265.66	56	$256,331.48
32	$35,808.26	57	$275,558.69
33	$39,598.84	58	$296,131.80
34	$43,654.76	59	$318,145.02
35	$47,994.59	**60**	**$341,699.17**
36	$52,638.21	61	$366,902.12
37	$57,606.89	62	$393,869.26
38	$62,923.37	63	$422,724.11
39	$68,612.00	**64**	**$453,598.80**
40	**$74,698.85**		

I can hear the complaints all the way from Jefferson City, Missouri. "But Mr. Wufot, how can I save $100 per month?" It's actually easy if you apply yourself. Plus, if you discipline yourself early in life to save $100 per month, then later in life, as you start making more money, you can save a lot more per month and possibly save into the millions.

Top JOBS For TEENS—don't be too proud to work

- » Fast food industry
- » Babysitter
- » Lawn and garden care
- » Grocery store
- » Department store
- » Hardware store
- » Coffee barista
- » Newspaper delivery or printing press
- » Clean and detail cars
- » Tutor
- » Waiter
- » Taxi or other car delivery services
- » Delivery food driver by bike or car
- » Farmworker
- » House and office cleaning
- » Camp counselor

» Janitor

» Concrete factory

» Cell phone store

» Gym or swimming pool

» Movie theatre

» Ice skating rink

» Museum

» Bowling alley

» Hotel reception

» Catering

» DJ or music artist

» Music lessons

» Umpire sporting events

» Nursing Home

My goal with this month's newsletter is to provide you with a framework to help you obtain your first job. I can give advice and motivation all day long, but it is up to you to get out there and make it happen. Be a doer!!! May the power of compounding interest be with you,

Baron Wufot

Since Baron Wufot had already done all of the heavy lifting, I decided the next thing I needed to do was write a resume. The only problem was that I didn't have any work experience

except for the time I helped Baron Wufot's tech team put together the app for the stock market competition. But I still only had one measly job to put on my resume.

Then it came to me! I came up with this brilliant idea to make up a fake resume. Now, hear me out. The plan was to make up a fictional resume as if I was five years older. The resume would reflect the work experience I hoped to have in five years. Of course, I was not trying to deceive anybody and I planned on putting a note at the top or bottom of my resume saying to the extent that I was actually sixteen years old with no real work experience. The resume would actually reflect the vision I have for my career path over the next five years. Instead of handing the potential employer a blank piece of paper, I would be candid about developing this "resume of the future" to give them an idea of the direction I plan to take in my life.

Then another idea came to me: I could use Baron Wufot's list of potential jobs for teenagers and pick out the top ten jobs I wanted. When choosing my top ten jobs, I took into consideration two things: the closeness of the job's location to my house and the jobs for which I actually felt qualified. Because this was my first time applying for a job, I didn't think I could be too selective. I just needed to make some money and get into the game.

Here is the process I developed to get my first job.

Step 1: Make a list of your top ten job choices.

STL Movie Theater, Paddle Department Store, Luck's Grocery Store, The City Museum, Home Improvement Store, Neutron Coffee, LMAO Pizza, Luminosity Electronic Store, Hotel Chariot, St. Louis Gateway Arch

Step 2: Pick up job applications.

When picking up the application, always ask for the hiring manager's name and when he/she will be working next. You will never get a job if you do not meet the hiring manager in person. So make sure to write down the hiring manager's name and the next time that he/she will be working.

Step 3: Prepare your fictional resume (if you do not have a resume).

How can you develop a resume if you don't have any job experience? I came up with this crazy idea to create a fictional resume that reflects my vision for my career path over the next five years. Make sure to make a note at the top or bottom of the page in bold letters, **"This resume is the career path I envision taking. It would be an honor to begin my career with [insert company name here]."**

At first, I was hesitant to use this idea. But as I began interviewing with hiring managers and telling them about the idea of sharing the vision of my career path with them, they loved the idea. I got three job offers on the spot. Dare to be different! It will help you stand out among other applicants.

Step 4: Make ten separate resumes.

This is easier than it sounds. To do this, make one resume and change the job on each resume to reflect the job for which you are applying. It's super easy to create a template in a spreadsheet.

For example:

Resume 1:

Franklin Fi

St. Louis, Missouri

(314) 828-9xxx

STL Movie Theater: Ticket Sales and Concessions
(2019-2021)—St. Louis, Missouri

> » Cleaned and maintained the exterior and interior of the theater including the auditoriums and restrooms

> » Took pride in displaying excellent guest service skills

This is slot one on your resume. It is the one you change depending on what job you are applying for.

Camp of the Ozarks: Camp Counselor
(2021)—Potosi, Missouri

> » Designed and implemented a weekly activity schedule for 8 campers

University of Missouri: Computer Lab Technician
(2021-2025)—Columbia, Missouri

> » Provided student support and customer service

> » Knowledgeable in current operating systems and software applications

Baltimore Pirates: Marketing Intern
(2020 Internship)—Baltimore, Maryland

> » Assisted the Marketing Director of a professional football team

The Umbrella Brokerage Company: Sales Intern
(2021 Internship)—San Francisco, California

- » Selected as the first intern on the trading desk in 10 years
- » Supported two managing partners with their stock market order flow

UBU Investment Bank: Sales and Trading Intern
(2022 Internship)—Manhattan, New York

- » Selected from a pool of 500 candidates over a 3-day interview process
- » Interned on the world's largest trading floor

Jack Wilson Partners: Institutional Sales Director
(2023-2033)—San Francisco, California

- » Worked as an associate broker on the trading floor
- » Facilitated institutional order flow, buybacks, and IPOs
- » Obtained Series 7 and 63 to become a Financial Broker

Note: I am applying for my first job and I have no job experience. The above resume is the vision I have for my career path, and I created this resume to exhibit my passion for entering the workforce.

Resume 2:

Franklin Fi
St. Louis, Missouri
(314) 828-9xxx

Paddle Department Store: Sales Associate
(2019-2021)—St. Louis, Missouri

» Provided top-notch customer service

» Provided top-notch customer service (This is not a misprint. Customer service was my #1 priority.)

» Stocked shelves, maintained a clean work environment, and performed cashier responsibilities

This is slot one on your resume. It is the one you change depending on what job you are applying for.

Camp of the Ozarks: Camp Counselor
(2021)—Potosi, Missouri

» Designed and implemented a weekly activity schedule for 8 campers

University of Missouri: Computer Lab Technician
(2021-2025)—Columbia, Missouri

» Provided student support and customer service

» Knowledgeable in current operating systems and software applications

Baltimore Pirates: Marketing Intern

(2020 Internship)—Baltimore, Maryland

» Assisted the Marketing Director of a professional football team

The Umbrella Brokerage Company: Sales Intern

(2021 Internship)—San Francisco, California

» Selected as the first intern on the trading desk in 10 years

» Supported two managing partners with their stock market order flow

UBU Investment Bank: Sales and Trading Intern

(2022 Internship)—Manhattan, New York

» Selected from a pool of 500 candidates over a 3-day interview process

» Interned on the world's largest trading floor

Jack Wilson Partners: Institutional Sales Director

(2023-2033)—San Francisco, California

» Worked as an associate broker on the trading floor

» Facilitated institutional order flow, buybacks, and IPOs

» Obtained Series 7 and 63 to become a Financial Broker

Note: I am applying for my first job and I have no job experience. The above resume is the vision I have for my career path, and I created this resume to exhibit my passion for entering the workforce.

Resume 3:

Luck's Grocery Store: Cashier
Etc.

Resume 4:

LMAO Pizza: Pie Tosser
Etc.

Resume 5:

Neutron Coffee: Barista
Etc.

You get the idea. The process was very simple once I put together the first version of my resume.

Finally, I wrote a cover letter explaining my situation: I am sixteen years old and applying for my first job. The attached resume actually reflects my vision for where I want to be in the next ten or fifteen years. Of course, I included important information in my cover letter, like I am extremely hardworking and willing to do just about anything to kickstart my career.

After a couple of hours working on my resume, I checked one last time for misspelled words and then hit print. I printed off ten copies of my resume and cover letter, each one tailored to the company I was applying for. I was ready to take over the solar system. Well, at least St. Louis.

That night before bed, I ironed two shirts. One for passing out resumes in the morning and one shirt for my hot date with Logi Laru later that night at the City Museum!

The next morning, I woke up around eight o'clock and had breakfast with my family. Breakfast in my household is like a dogfight over scraps of food. There's not a lot of food to go around in my house, so we don't hold back when there is food on the table. I have an older brother, an older sister, and a younger brother. Normally, that would mean I am safely insulated from hazing, but not this morning. Somehow, my older brother found out I was going on my first date in the whole history of my short life. Boy, did he let me have it! He offered to let me borrow his bike and asked me weird questions, like what does she smell like. He can be such a weirdo sometimes. Of course, it was all in good fun. I should have expected some brotherly hazing, but you can never be prepared for what an older brother is willing to unleash on you.

With my resumes packed away in a manila envelope and neatly placed in my backpack, I ran out the door and didn't look back.

The night before, I mapped out the most direct route to cycle to my potential employers. It was a piece of cake, Disco (my bike) and I hit all ten of them in a few hours and even had time to grab a hot salami sandwich from Gioia's Deli, the best sandwich shop on the Italian Hill in St. Louis.

Luckily, I even got to speak to the hiring managers at three of the businesses. The hiring manager at LMAO Pizza loved my initiative and offered me a weekend position in the kitchen.

The weekend manager at the Paddle Department Store said he loved my creativity and could tell I was a people person. He said it is impossible to find someone who can relate to people of all walks of life. He told me I have the gift of gab and he would give me a call on Monday to let me know how many hours he could scrape together for me.

Lastly, the manager at the downtown Hotel Chariot told me there was an opening for a night receptionist position and she invited me to come for an interview. I was on fire! The resumes were a huge hit with potential employers and I was on my way to landing my first job!

That Saturday morning, I knew I had taken my first steps to financial independence when I accepted the job at Paddle Department Store. They offered the most hours after school and during the weekends. Plus, they offered the best benefits. They even said they will pay up to $3,000 a year for my college once I graduated high school. Paddle offered $12/hour starting pay. Working 26 hours a week at $12/hour, I would make about $225 a week or $450 every two-week pay period after taxes.

My dream was starting to become a reality. I figured after working and saving for a month, I would have more than $500 stuffed away in a savings or investment account. My dad agreed to cosign on what they call a custodial brokerage account. Basically, someone over 18 years old must agree to act as the custodian or cosigner on the account. It was super easy.

In his newsletters, Baron Wufot wrote, if a sixteen-year-old started contributing $100 a month until retirement, that monthly contribution would one day be worth over $450,000, assuming retirement at the age of 64.

By downloading a compound interest app on my cell phone, I figured in order to have over a million dollars at retirement, I needed to save $250 per month from the age of 16 to 64. With compound interest, I could save $1,178,979 by retirement, assuming the historical market average rate of return of 7%.

Now, I tell everybody to download a compound interest app and play around with it. Every time I save or contribute money to the stock market, I figure out my compound interest and what it may be worth at retirement. This is pure motivation to save more money.

8

First Date

That Saturday was quite possibly the best day of my life. I secured my first job and I went on my first date with Logi. All of my hard work and positivity was paying off.

True to form, I arrived fifteen minutes early to the City Museum. It's truly a bad habit of mine to show up fifteen minutes early and the other person is typically ten to fifteen minutes late. This means I regularly spend a half an hour waiting for the other person.

"Hey, Logi! I'm over here!" I shouted as I waved my hands like a madman. I was a little excited to say the least. It wasn't like she was going to leave if she didn't see me.

"Hey, Fi! How's it going?" Logi greeted me.

"I got a job!" I told her with excitement. I told her how I concocted the idea of creating fake resumes and how I landed a job.

"You're a maniac, but a brilliant maniac! What possessed you to think of creating fake resumes? Who does that?" she asked.

"All I have been able to think about for the past few months is getting a job in order to invest in the stock market," I began to explain. "I knew the first step of getting a job was going to be the most difficult task. I had in my mind that I would be too proud to ask someone for a job, that I would get embarrassed and procrastinate, so I told myself I would pick up job applications next week. After going through the process for the last few weeks, I, with all of that pent-up energy, came up with this brilliant idea of making fictitious resumes. You should have seen the hiring managers when I showed them my fictitious resume and explained it to them. They responded like I invented sliced bread or the wheel. They couldn't believe a kid could come up with such a brilliant idea and have the initiative to execute the plan. Honestly, I don't think I would have ever thought up the plan if it wasn't for Baron Wufot's newsletter listing all of the possible jobs for a teen. It's so cool the Baron takes time to write the newsletter for us."

"Yeah, but the fake resumes was your idea," Logi added. "I don't know of anybody else on earth who would have thought of that idea. Franklin, don't sell yourself short by giving Baron Wufot all of the credit."

"Yeah, I guess you're right," I told her as I grabbed her hand. "Enough jabbering, let's go have some fun! It's been too long since I have been to the City Museum and I love this place." At that point, it occurred to me that I was holding Logi's hand. I was holding a girl's hand. A real girl, not some fake girl from my imagination!!!

The City Museum is practically the coolest place in the solar system, maybe even the galaxy! Someone had this insane idea to buy the old St. Louis Shoelace Factory and turn it into a four-story jungle gym. Basically, it's a huge playground for both kids and adults. The inside of the old factory is one big maze made up of tunnels, slides, ropes, half-pipes, and fireman poles for sliding down. The outside of the museum reminds me of that old board game "Mousetrap," only life-sized. You can run around and play on three stories of steel bridges, tunnels, ropes, and climbing walls that are all suspended high in the air. At the top, you can look down below and see all of the people crawling around through the jungle gym and tunnels. The best part is that it turns adults into kids again. You see grandparents chasing after their grandkids as if they were the same age. The City Museum is a blast!

"That's too bad that Malibu and Smooth already had plans," I said.

"Yeah, I thought if I could get them to hang out and have some fun together, then maybe they would loosen up a bit," Logi stated. "There are not a lot of people at our school I can relate to. Those two guys truly see me for who I am. High school is fun and all, but it's not going to be long before we graduate and start college."

All of this was said as we ducked and weaved through the mazes of the museum.

"What are your plans for college? Have you put much thought into it?" I asked Logi.

"Nothing is set in stone, but I was thinking of applying to the Journalism School at the University of Missouri. They have one of the best journalism schools in the country and it is only a couple of hours away from St. Louis. But, I guess it all comes down to my SAT score," Logi said.

"That sounds like a good plan, you are an awesome writer," I told her. "I didn't realize you wanted to be a journalist, but it makes sense now that I think about it."

"My dream has always been to travel the world and cover the different types of spirituality around the world. There's so much negativity being covered in the news today. I want a career that presents the world as a positive stream of information. I want to give people hope all over the world and unite people of all ages, races, and religions." Logi continued. "My parents would die if they knew my plans. They worked so hard to move here from India and become doctors. I'm certain they would think I was crazy for wanting to take off and travel. They have worked to give me everything they did not have as kids. Can you imagine what they would think about me wanting to return to the type of life they abandoned?"

"I wouldn't worry too much about it. You are years away from fulfilling your dream. Don't get too worked up over it, we've still got a good five or six years before we hit the full-time labor force," I assured Logi.

"What about you, Franklin Fi? Mr. Teenage-Financial Genius, what are your plans for college?" Logi asked with a smack on my knee.

Oh my gosh, is she flirting with me? I thought to myself. *SHE SMACKED MY KNEE! Does that count as getting to first base?* I was shaking and didn't know what to do. *Do I smack her knee back?*

"Uh, well, uh, you know, I haven't put much thought into college," I said, but that was the furthest thing from the truth. I had actually put a lot of thought into college. I collected myself and continued. "Unfortunately, I don't think I am going to be lucky enough to get a scholarship; my grades just aren't good enough. I have a bad habit of spending too much time studying the things I am interested in like finance, and not enough time on my school work. Plus, being one of four kids in my family, I don't think my parents are going to be able to help me out with college."

"What about student loans?" Logi asked, though I am sure she already knew what my answer was going to be.

"There is no way I am going in debt to go to a major university. I've seen too many of my cousins get caught in that trap. Then, they would realize they would spend the next twenty years paying off student loans. My cousin told me he has $40,000 in student loans and it looks like it will take more than twenty years for him to pay it off. Research shows that it takes a recent college grad a long time to repay his or her loans. To think, these people are supposed to be smart for going to college, but all they have done is enslave themselves for the next twenty years."

"Franklin Freakin Fi, you are too smart not to go to college!" she scolded me like I was her son, using my full name and all!

"Oh, I am definitely going to college," I informed her. "My plan is to work part-time and go to a community college here in St. Louis. Hopefully, after two years I will transfer to a four-year university like the University of Missouri. But I just refuse to go in debt. I plan on working through college to get ahead. What I really would like is to continue to learn how to invest and spend my college years building a strong investment portfolio. My goal is to graduate college with savings in the bank, instead of $40,000 in debt. Also, like you, one day I would love to travel abroad and maybe even live in another country for a while. I like St. Louis and all, but there has to be more out there than this. Although, the City Museum is pretty freakin' rad."

"My friend, you are wise beyond your years. Where do

you come up with this stuff? This is all coming from the same guy that just concocted a fake resume scheme to land a job today," she said with a look of admiration in her eyes. I love how Indian people always say "my friend." It makes me feel awesome every time I hear them say it.

"Careful, I fully disclosed my fake resume to every potential employer. I don't want you to think I cheated. What was I supposed to do...walk in there with a blank sheet of paper for my resume? Can you imagine the hiring manager's face if I handed them a blank sheet of paper with only my name and address on the top of it?" I joked. "Honestly, the Baron is to blame for this behavior. He's the one who inspired a lot of my crazy ideas. He writes in his newsletter "to think a little differently and do things just a little smarter than the next person." He's right. It is stupid for everyone to keep doing the same things as everyone else. It's evolution and I plan to continue to forge my own path hopefully in a manner that has never been done before. It's kind of like a video game; we're all just walking around this world picking up tools and treasures that will help us in the future. If you think of it that way, then it becomes a grand adventure. How do you get to the next level? Well, you acquire the tools that are necessary to help you defeat an opponent to reach an end goal. Stop me if none of this is making sense."

"Oh, I hear you, Franklin. I'm just curious to know what tool or treasure you are pursuing tonight." Logi questioned me with a big smile on her face.

Who knew Logi Laru was so good at flirting? I had known Logi for years and she has never said stuff like this to me before. Though, until now, we had not really spent all that much time alone. I couldn't figure out if she was really flirting with me or if I was just making it up in my head. I'm horrible at reading girls' intentions. Unfortunately, I always get ahead of myself and think every girl is madly in love with me, just because they said something nice to me.

"Uh, I hadn't really thought about it being a treasure hunt tonight. But I guess there is not a better place for a treasure hunt than a four-story jungle gym. Let's head over to the outside playground and see what kind of treasures we can find out there," I flirted back. "Enough of all of this serious talk about college and working. Shouldn't we be living in the present right now, Miss Laru?"

For the next hour or so, we chased each other around the City Museum like we were eight years old again. It felt so good to be around a friend and not have to pretend about anything. It didn't hurt that she was the girl of my dreams and the most amazing person in the solar system. She definitely had a hold on me.

Before we knew what happened, the lights dimmed in the City Museum. It was a sign the museum was closing and we needed to leave. I took it as a sign from the heavens and leaned in for a kiss! No, not really. I wish. If I could do a replay, I totally should have taken it as a sign to go in for the kiss. But I wasn't certain I was reading the clues correctly.

"Do you need a ride home? I am happy to call us a cab to get you home safely," I told Logi. St. Louis really isn't the safest city at eleven o'clock on a Saturday night. Plus, I really wanted to spend some more time with Logi.

"Cool, that's nice of you, Franklin," Logi replied. "My dad said to call him if I needed a ride, but I am sure he's fine with me catching a taxi with a friend. I'll shoot him a quick text. Can we split the taxi fare?"

"Are you kidding me! You are talking to the newly employed Franklin Fi! I'll get the taxi tonight and you can get the next one," I told her. I was already planting the seed in her mind for another date. Wow, my courage was through the roof, I had practically already asked her on another date. Practically!

"Thanks for a great night, Franklin," she told me as we passed through downtown St. Louis in the taxi.

"Yeah, I had a blast. I think I could go to the City Museum every night for the rest of my life. I love that place!" I exclaimed.

"We should totally invite Smooth and Malibu next time. I can't believe those guys skipped out on us," Logi said cheerfully, (too cheerfully I thought). What was her fascination with Smooth and Malibu?

"For sure," I said as my heart sank. Why are girls so hard to figure out? Just when I thought I had Logi figured out, she brushes me off with a curveball I wasn't expecting. Does she like Smooth or Malibu or does she just want us all to be better friends? Why can't people just say what they are thinking? Wait! That would mean I would have to say what I am thinking. And there is no way I have the nerve right now to confess my feelings to Logi.

"Thanks for getting me home," Logi said as she came straight for my face. She's going to kiss me, I thought. She's headed straight for me. Sheesh, she's going for it. What am I supposed to do? At the last second, she veered off to the right and gave me a kiss on my cheek. Sweet baby, hey Zeus! That was close. I actually thought I was going to make it to first base tonight. But nooo, she came back at me with an inside slider and caught me off balance. What's wrong with girls. I wonder if they know how crazy they make us men feel?

"Night Logi, I had a great time. I'll see you at school on Monday. Oh, and have fun finding those P/E ratios for your stocks," I said as she got out of the taxi. As the taxi sped away, it occurred to me that the last thing I said to Logi was about finding those P/E ratios, as in those Price to Earnings Ratios. How dumb was I? Of all the things I could have said! I am such a freaking idiot. She was flirting with me all night and I didn't have the nerve to go in for a kiss. Such a fool! It really sucks having feelings for someone and not knowing what to do about it. I just get all confused when it comes to talking with Logi. Then I fall apart and say something stupid about P/E ratios. Does she even like me or does she like Smooth or Malibu? I wonder if she feels the same way I do? These thoughts were swimming in my head as I rode home alone in the taxi.

9

Pay Yourself First

Baron Wufot's
Personal Finance Newsletter for Teens
November 1

What's your number?

What do I mean by "What's your number?" That could mean anything. What's your age? How much money do you make? Well, this time, I am referring to your budget. Or, how much can you afford to spend until the next pay period or month. I have a monthly budget and then I divide that number by thirty to get my daily budget. For example, I remember when my daily budget used to be five dollars a day. This number should be a stretch or a difficult number for you to stay within.

I am always amazed by how 99.9% of the people on this planet walk around spending money without knowing what they can afford to spend. They have no clue what a budget is. They don't know "what their number is."

Ask yourself this: How much money did you spend last month or even yesterday? I'm guessing you probably don't have the slightest clue. Doesn't everyone want to be rich? If this is true, then why don't most people know how much they're spending? I guarantee a large majority of wealthy people know exactly how much money they spent last month because that is part of accumulating wealth. They know how important it is to understand how much money is coming in (income) and how much money is going out (expenses). They live their lives like they are running a business. They see their lives as a "human corporation."

Most people receive one to two paychecks a month, so income is easy to calculate. For example, if you get paid $1,000 twice a month, you are making $2,000/month. No problem, we can all figure that out. This money is income or revenue.

Figuring out your income is the easy part. The hard part is figuring out how much you are spending and where the money is going. Once you have calculated it a couple of times, it's pretty much a no-brainer. Most people are afraid to find out how much money they are wasting on things they don't necessarily need or use.

When you receive your paycheck, hopefully you pay all of your outstanding debts or bills. You might pay off your cell phone bill, make your car payment, pay rent if you have already moved out of your parent's house, and then make the minimum payment on your credit card bill. Before you know it, you have spent most of your paycheck to pay your bills. In other words, you have paid off everybody except yourself. There is hardly anything left over to enjoy the money you have earned. Unfortunately, the trap you may fall into is using your credit card again to hold you over to the next paycheck. And this is how people fall further and further into debt.

There are two problems with this common scenario. First, you continue to fall deeper and deeper in debt. Second, you have paid everybody else but not yourself. Paying yourself means saving or investing your hard-earned money so it can be available to you in the future. If you are not paying yourself, this is a real problem. What's the point of working if you can't make enough to enjoy life, and make an investment in your future or retirement?

Here's how the scenario plays out in a Profit and Loss Statement for the average American:

The Average American's Profit and Loss Statement

November 1st—30th

Income:

Paycheck 1 (Nov 1)	$1,000
Paycheck 2 (Nov 15)	$1,000
Total Income	**$2,000**

Expenses:

Mortgage on House	$700
Groceries	$400
Car Loan (car pmt, gas, insurance, etc.)	$400
Restaurants and other entertainment	$300
TV, Internet, and Cell phone	$200
Credit Card Bill	$200
Utilities	$150
Clothing	$100
Coffee Shop Donation	$100
Total Expenses	**$2,550**

Total Income — Total Expenses = Profit or Loss
$2,000 — $2,550 = $550
(that's a loss of $550 for the month!)

Problem 1 with the Average American's Profit and Loss Statement

You have successfully managed to lose $550. In other words, you spent $550 more than you made that month. This is not a sustainable lifestyle. What is scary about this scenario is that the majority of Americans are living this way. So where do you get the extra $550 you spent? You put it on a credit card that charges you 18% interest, which works out to $100 in interest for every $550 you borrow on a credit card. You are paying the bank $100 for every $550 you charge on a credit card. The banks really like taking your money or finding creative ways to loan you money so they can collect interest on your loans or debt.

Now think about this: The average American owes about $6,000 in credit card debt. Another way to say this is, at an 18% interest rate the average American is paying the banks over $1,000 a year to borrow money from them. Does paying thousands of dollars to borrow money from the banks sound like a good deal to you? Most teens probably don't have any debt yet. But now is the time to start learning about debt. It is only a matter of time before the banks start coming for you, and you need to know what to do when that time comes.

Problem 2 with the Average American's Profit and Loss Statement

You have gone in debt to pay everybody else but yourself. What's the point of working if you are just paying off debt you have incurred in prior weeks or months? It just doesn't make sense. Another frightening statistic: roughly 70% of Americans who died last year were on average $60,000 in debt. That's right! Seven out of ten Americans are in debt when they die. This means that seven out of ten Americans will work practically their whole life paying off debt and die with significant debt. Don't fall into this trap!

ALWAYS PAY YOURSELF FIRST!!!

How do you pay yourself first? The very second you receive a paycheck, go straight to the bank or transfer a large percentage of your paycheck to a savings account that is not readily accessible. Make it automatic! Don't pay anybody else until you pay yourself. Then, pay your bills. The remainder of money after paying yourself and everyone else is your spending budget for the rest of the pay period. This is what rich people do, it's no secret to them.

1. Pay yourself by putting money into a brokerage or savings account. If you are in debt and think you don't have any money to save, then start by saving a small amount like $50 or $100 per month. It will start to add up faster than you could have realized.

2. Pay your bills...always.

3. The leftover amount is your spending budget. You can not spend more than this amount or you are incurring debt.

Now let's look at what a financially intelligent person's Profit and Loss Statement looks like:

The Intelligent American's Profit and Loss Statement

November 1st—30th

Income:

Paycheck 1 (Nov 1)	$1,000
Paycheck 2 (Nov 15)	$1,000
Total Income	**$2,000**

Expenses:

Housing (downsize or live with roommates)	$400
Groceries (only eat at home, budget $50/week)	$200
Transportation (ride a bike or take the bus)	$100
Restaurants and other entertainment $45/week)	$180
TV, Internet, and Cell phone (No TV or internet)	$50
Credit Card Payments (don't own one)	$0
Utilities (smaller house or split with roommates)	$70
Clothing (buy new clothes once a year, if needed)	$0
Coffee Shop Donation (unnecessary expense)	$0
Total Expenses	**$1000**

Total Income — Total Expenses = Profit or Loss
$2,000 — $1,000 = $1,000 profit or amount you can save per month

Pay yourself first: If you get paid twice a month, immediately deposit $500 on Nov. 1 and $500 on Nov. 15 for a total of $1,000 per month.

First, let me tell you, this is very possible. I used to save over 50% of my paycheck when I first started saving. All you have to do is think outside of the box a little bit and get creative with your housing, transportation, entertainment, cell phone, and TV/internet expenses. The good news, as a teen you may not have some of these expenses. Every teen who is receiving a paycheck should be saving over 50% of what they earn. Start this habit when you are young and make it a habit for a lifetime. Don't let yourself get behind or fall into debt.

The above Profit and Loss Statement is very possible and really a matter of consciously deciding you want to save money—that you want to get ahead and possibly achieve Financial Independence (FI) one day.

In this scenario, you actually save $1,000 or 50% of your paycheck. I know you are saying this is impossible. Well, start by making your own personal Profit and Loss Statement and see where you stand.

GOOD NEWS

If you are reading this newsletter, you are probably in your teens and your Profit and Loss Statement is going to look a lot differently. For starters, your housing, utilities, groceries, and possibly even your transportation expenses are going to be a big fat ZERO. Right now, go give your mom and dad a big kiss and thank them for paying for these expenses. You might think these things are free, but they are not. Your parents are paying a lot of money to raise you, so show your appreciation. Not everybody in the world is as fortunate to have parents that provide these things for you. You are one lucky kid, so please make sure to show your appreciation.

Now, let's see what a teen's Profit and Loss Statement might look like.

The Teenager's Profit and Loss Statement

November 1st—30th

Income:

Paycheck 1 (Nov 1)	$400
Paycheck 2 (Nov 15)	$400
Total Income	**$800**

Expenses:

Housing or rent	$0
Groceries	$0
Transportation (car pmt, gas, insurance, etc.)	$50
Restaurants and other entertainment	$100
TV, Internet, and Cell phone	$50
Credit Card Payments	$0
Utilities	$0
Clothing	$100
Coffee Shop Donation	$0
Total Expenses	**$300**

Total Income — Total Expenses = Profit or Loss
$800 — $300 = $500 profit

In this scenario, I would put $250 into my savings account or brokerage account on November 1st and then again on November 15th for a total of $500 saved for the month. That is a savings rate of 63%, which can simply be found by dividing your total profit by your total income. In this case, $500 ÷ $800 equals 63%.

Total Profit ÷ Total Income = Savings Rate

Teens have a huge advantage because they don't have to pay for a lot of their expenses. Take advantage of this opportunity to get ahead and stay ahead. Don't let this opportunity pass you by. Go out there and get a job. For the rest of your life, you will thank yourself. Make it a goal of yours to become a saver and to work towards financial independence. Believe it or not, you can be a successful investor, even as a teenager. Achieving financial independence may be more difficult as you get older and older if you have not formed good habits at an early age. Just start saving, even $20 or $100 a month. Get in the game!

Now let's have some fun. Let's look at a scenario when compound interest is applied.

Given:
Starting Value: $0
Monthly contribution: $500
Time: 44 yrs to retirement
Savings rate: 7% (historical market average is 7%)

Value at Retirement: $1,762,677

All of my calculations can be done on a compounding interest app that you can download on your cell phone or on your computer. These apps are very easy to find and download.

How about that? You can save $1.7 million just by investing $500 a month for the rest of your life. How does that sound?

Okay, okay, I can hear you all the way from Jefferson City, Missouri. You think you can't save $500 a month. Well, then let's look at how much you would have if you were able to save $100 a month for the rest of your life and invested it in the stock market.

Given:
Starting Value: $0
Monthly contribution: $100
Time: 44 yrs to retirement
Savings rate: 7% (historical market average is 7%)

Value at Retirement: $352,535

All of my calculations can be done on a compounding interest app that you can download on your cell phone or on your computer. These apps are very easy to find and download.

I will say that every teenager reading this newsletter can save $100 a month. In fact, accept the challenge. It is a matter of deciding what you want, then doing it. Saving $100 is very attainable if you go about it in a disciplined manner.

Just for fun, let's look at one more example. Let's look at how much money you can save if you contribute $200 a month.

Given:
Starting Value: $0
Monthly contribution: $200
Time: 44 yrs to retirement
Savings rate: 7% (historical market average is 7%)

Value at Retirement: $705,071
All of my calculations can be done on a compounding interest app that you can download on your cell phone or on your computer. These apps are very easy to find and download.

This should be all the motivation you need to start saving. If you are already saving, this should be motivation to challenge yourself to save more and more every month. As a teenager, you have a very good chance to achieve financial independence, if you start saving early.

Now, for the moment you have all been waiting for! Here are the **current standings** for the High School Stock Market Competition after two weeks.

Update: High School Stock Market Competition—November

	Name	Total	City, State
1.	SmallCapWonder	$11,007.23	New York, NY
2.	Smootherrific	$10,904.92	St. Louis, MO
3.	Mago de Wall St.	$10,756.12	Miami, FL
4.	Bearless	$10,723.87	Sheboygan, WI
5.	TheBull	$10,717.34	Seattle, WA

4,347 students from around the country entered the competition. Not bad for the first annual BW's High School Stock Market Competition! Hopefully, this means there are 4,347 students who want to better themselves by learning about the stock market and personal finance.

Thank you all for entering and don't give up! There are more than five months of the competition left. The $10,000 prize is still anybody's to win!

This has been a Baron Wufot Production. Remember, kiddos, pick 'em to hold 'em and let compound interest do the rest.

Your friend,
Baron Wufot

"Have you all seen Baron Wufot's November newsletter?" Smooth shouted as he ran into room #244 where the Stock

Market Club is held. "Who's the baddest? Who's the raddest? Mr. Smoothtastic, so very fantastic!"

We had all just arrived for the monthly Stock Market Club meeting. Obviously, Smooth was excited. He just found out he was in second place out of more than four thousand participants in the national stock market competition.

"Representing the 314!" Malibu said, referring to St. Louis's area code. He jumped up and gave Smooth a high five as they both jumped as high as they could. It looked like the opening tip-off of a basketball game between a chubby penguin and a miniature pinscher dog.

"I wonder who SmallCapWonder from New York, NY is?" I questioned.

"I don't know, but he must have a small head or maybe he is a freshman? Why else would he call himself 'small hat wonder'?" Smooth speculated out loud.

"Smooth, I think he is referring to the type of stocks he likes to invest in," Logi answered. "That would be the logical answer."

"Oh, really," Smooth said. "I just thought the person was referring to their small head size. You know what they say about people with small heads?"

"No, what do they say about people with small heads?" I asked.

"Oh, I don't know either. I was asking you," Smooth came back at me.

"I'm going to have to agree with Logi on this one. I think that person's screen name is referring to the type of stock he or she likes to invest in," I continued. "A small cap stock is a company that has a market capitalization less than $2 billion, which is, believe it or not, a small company."

"What flavor of Baron Wufot's magic potion are you trying to peddle us today, Franklin? You're telling me a small cap company is $2 billion or smaller. That seems awfully big to me. How do you find the company's 'market hat'?" Smooth questioned.

"That's 'small cap' as in capitalization. It's actually very easy to find a company's market capitalization. All you do is multiply the company's stock price by the number of shares outstanding.

For example, Chocolate Cake Inc. is trading at $37 per share and has 10 million shares in existence. What is the market capitalization for Chocolate Cake Inc.?

$$\$37 \times 10{,}000{,}000 \text{ shares} = \$370{,}000{,}000$$

Small cap companies are considered to be a little bit riskier than medium and large cap companies for the fact that they are smaller companies and the largest investors tend to stay away from them."

"You mean to tell me a company worth $370,000,000 is considered a small company? I have never even counted that high!" Smooth claimed.

"So what's a big head company?" Malibu Martin joked with us.

"You're getting ahead of your head sizes. Let's first look at what makes a mid cap company. A mid cap company has a market cap between $2 billion and $10 billion," I explained to them. "That means a large cap company is anything over $10 billion. A good example of a large cap company is Doctor and Ramble Corporation."

Small Capitalization Companies = $300 million to $2 billion
Mid Capitalization Companies = $2 billion to $10 billion
Large Capitalization Companies = $10 billion and up

"Large cap stocks tend to carry the least amount of risk because they are well-established companies with a long track record. But like most things in the stock market, risk can be hard to gauge. There are a lot of factors that make some companies riskier than others," I told them.

"Layers upon layers upon layers," Malibu Martin said in his froggy voice. "This stock market stuff is some complicated business. So you're telling me, the cheaper the stock price, the riskier the stock is, and the possibility of a higher rate of return on my investment?"

"More or less," I answered. "There are even stocks called 'penny stocks' that are worth mere pennies. Penny stocks are super risky and are kind of like gambling. Sometimes, they can triple in a day and then go to zero the next day. It's an easy way to lose everything when you invest in penny stocks."

"Sounds like my kind of investment," said Malibu Martin. "So you're telling me I can triple my virtual portfolio of $10,000 by investing in penny stocks?"

"Yeah, there is a very slim chance that might happen. But, there is an even better chance you could lose everything because the company trading as a penny stock could easily go bankrupt. The reason a company is a penny stock is usually because they are losing way more money than they are making."

Malibu wasn't doing that badly in the competition. He was right around 200th place, which was pretty amazing considering there were over four thousand kids competing in the competition. Logi and I were somewhere in the middle. We both put together pretty conservative portfolios, using the competition more as a learning experience than anything else. Don't get me wrong, I would love to win the competition but I was not going to start gambling with my virtual portfolio to win. My investment strategy was owning value-growth stocks and I was sticking to it. Logi was half invested in the S&P 500 index, which she expected to be less volatile than most other investments. I kind of got the feeling Logi's parents had been contributing money to a college savings account that was invested in the stock market. She was in learning mode, just like me.

"Okay, let's focus and get to work on our homework," I stated. "Who researched the P/E ratios of the companies they invested in?"

"My hamster ate my homework!" Smooth said with a laugh. "Nah, just joking!"

"Really, I thought you were serious, your royal smoothness," Malibu quipped back.

Surprisingly, everybody remembered to do their homework. It was awesome. We all compared notes and this is roughly the definition we all decided on for P/E ratio:

The **price** to **earnings ratio** (**P/E ratio**) is the **ratio** for valuing a company that measures its **current share price** relative to its per-share **earnings.**

Earnings per share (EPS) is the portion of a company's **profit** allocated to each **outstanding share** of common stock. Earnings per share serves as an indicator of a company's profitability.

Price per share ÷ Earnings per Share = P/E ratio

Example:
Price per Share = $30
Earnings per Share = $3

$30 ÷ $3 = 10 P/E ratio

Therefore, an investor is willing to pay $10 for every $1 of earnings.

Note:

- » P/E ratio less than or equal to zero indicates an **unprofitable** company

  - P/E ratio ≤ 0 = unprofitable company

- » P/E ratio from zero to twenty is considered a **value stock** most of the time and that it is possibly underpriced

  - P/E ratio from 0 to 20 = value stock and possibly underpriced

- » P/E ratio greater than twenty is considered a **growth stock** most of the time

  - P/E ratio > 20 = growth stock with the possibility of being an overpriced company

The P/E ratio can be easily found on any financial website that lists financial information for a company. Just search online for the company's stock price and then look under the tab "key statistics" or "key ratios."

"I found my technology stocks had really high P/E ratios, like in the 50s and 60s," Malibu Martin stated.

"Good work and that makes sense," I told him. "Technology

stocks are known as growth stocks, which means that some investors are willing to pay more for their stock based on the possibility of higher future earnings. Basically, you are paying for earnings that have not happened yet. Some investors base their whole portfolios on growth stocks, whereas **value investors** are more conservative and like to invest in stocks with low P/E ratios. A low P/E ratio means that company has higher earnings or profits relative to the stock price."

"My stocks were pretty mixed," Smooth added. "Half of my stocks were around a P/E ratio of 15x to 20x, and the other half of my portfolio had P/E ratios in the 30s, 40s, and 50s."

"So you have a mix of value stocks and growth stocks," I informed him.

"Most of my stocks were value stocks," Logi added.

"Same here. We tend to be on the conservative side when it comes to investing," I said. "I'm having a hard time switching up my investment style for this short-term competition, because it's only six months long. According to Baron Wufot, successful investors invest in value stocks you plan on holding for the rest of your life. I told myself that investing virtual funds in this competition would be a good opportunity to put that theory to the test before I start investing with my real money."

"Unlike you, brother man, I've got the stomach for risk," Malibu cut in. "I'm in it to win it. I am going to look into some of those penny stocks. I don't even know why I have been wasting my time on these conservative stocks."

"Technology stocks or growth stocks with high P/E ratios aren't considered to be conservative. Penny stocks are super risky compared to growth stocks, so be careful," I warned, "but what do you have to lose? We are investing virtual money.

Your way of learning is just as good as mine. It'll be interesting to see who comes out on top."

"I don't know about you, but I plan on winning the $10,000 prize. The way I see it, the only way to do that is to go big or go home," Malibu Martin reinforced his position.

"I'm not getting all crazy, but I think I am going to sell my two worst stocks and put that virtual money into my two top-performing stocks in my portfolio," Smooth strategized.

"That literally sounds like a smooth move, Smooth. As in, that sounds like a smart investment strategy, verging on brilliant!" Logi said. "I think I am going to give my portfolio one more month before I start moving things around. But I like your idea!"

"They don't call you Logical Laru for nothing," Malibu croaked like a frog.

"Good stuff. We got a lot done today," I said to the group. "We read over the latest newsletter from Baron Wufot on Profit and Loss Statements and discussed the P/E ratios of the companies we have in our virtual portfolios. What do you think about each of us putting together a personal Profit and Loss Statement for next month's meeting?"

"Dude, you would make a great teacher. You can give homework with the best of 'em!" Malibu Martin joked.

"I think it is a great idea to put together a personal Profit and Loss Statement for ourselves," Logi stated. "So we will all track our income and expenses for the month and then figure out if we are personally operating at a profit or loss?"

"Yeah, that's what I had in mind. It really won't take that long. Plus, I think we all stand to benefit from this exercise," I said.

"Alright, count me in," Malibu Martin agreed. "I just

have one question. I don't have a job, but my parents give me a monthly allowance for mowing the lawn and doing the dishes. Does my allowance count as income?"

"Sure does, you lucky punk!" I told him.

"I am excited about this little exercise," Logi said.

"Yeah, me too! I think we are all going to learn a lot about our personal spending habits. Until this point, we have just been wandering aimlessly through life, spending money when we have it. This is going to give us all a little more perspective on our lives. I can hardly wait to get started," I told them.

"Franklin, you have gone and drunk too much of the Baron's juice," Malibu Martin said. "Every time we start talking personal finance, you get all weird. It's like you are a kid who just found out you are going to Disney World. It's pure inspiration, man!"

"Yeah, I get pretty worked up when we talk about the stock market and making money," I replied. "It's like when you get back from Malibu and that's all you can talk about. You love Malibu like I love the stock market."

"Yeah, I can see that. I never thought about it that way, though. I definitely come back from Malibu, CA with a ton of energy," Malibu Martin confessed.

"Speaking of passions," Logi interrupted. "There is a disco yoga class on Saturday night. Would anybody like to join me?"

"FOR SURE, COUNT ME IN!" I shouted.

"Calm down, tiger. That was an awfully excited yes," Malibu joked. "Fortunately, I can't make it. I've got a date with a private school girl I have been trying to take out for months. Chicks, chicks, chicks!!!" Malibu started to dance and chant.

"What about you, Smooth?" Logi asked again.

"Um…yeah…well, it's my cousin's quinceañera on Saturday night, so I probably can't make it," Smooth stuttered.

"Dude, you're not even Mexican and you probably don't even know what that means," I told Smooth.

"My aunt is married to a guy from Mexico City," Smooth defended himself. "He throws the best parties. And, yes, I know what a quinceañera is. It is when a girl turns fifteen and all of her friends bring her gifts. Then, the parents have all of the fun and dance the night away. I've got smooooth moves that pay the bills, baby. You think I would miss a dance party for disco yoga? Sorry, Logi!"

"Whatever, Smooth. That is the worst lie I've ever heard," I told him.

"Looks like you two love doves have another date!" Smooth teased us and started to chant. "Yoda, Yoda, Yoda!!!"

It was ridiculous, Malibu was chanting "Chicks! Chicks! Chicks!" and Smooth was chanting "Yoda! Yoda! Yoda!" while they danced around each other trying to do the robot.

Brrrrriiiiinnnnggggggg!!! Brrrrriiiiinnnnggggggg!!!
Brrrrriiiiinnnnggggggg!!!

"Saved by the bell!" Logi said.

"Yeah, text me the details for disco yoga. As for you clowns, I'll see you on the flipside," I said as I rushed out of the room with a red face.

10

Disco Yoga

That Friday night, I met Logi at the hot yoga studio. She was wearing a neon pink, spandex catsuit that glowed in the dark. Logi looked freaking hot! I, on the other hand, had obviously not received the memo that said to dress like a psychedelic lunatic for disco yoga. I was wearing navy blue running shorts and a t-shirt that said "high on stress," which was actually pretty unfitting, considering that a yoga studio is usually a stress-free environment.

Disco yoga turned out to be a lot of fun. The first five minutes of class was completely dark and the only sound you could hear was the teacher's amplified breath. It was trippy! Then the strobe lights sporadically started flashing, the disco ball started spinning, and before you knew it, you were hot and heavy into a yoga routine choreographed to a Donna Summer's song. I realized quickly it didn't matter what I was wearing because we couldn't distinguish others in the room due to the chaos from the lights. The class was ninety minutes long in a heated room, so by the end of the class, my clothes were soaked with sweat from head to toe. We did some of the same poses Logi had been teaching us on the playground during lunch. Other than that, there were not many similarities. Disco yoga was much more about getting your heart rate up and making you sweat. Whereas the type of yoga Logi taught was much more fluid and peaceful.

After class let out, Logi and I headed to a cafe down the street for a cup of tea. She had a camomile tea, and I tried the African rooibos with ginger. Believe it or not, that was another first for me. I had never been to disco yoga and had never been out for tea. Sitting around and sipping on herbal teas was not a thing at the Fi household.

We sat and talked for what seemed like the whole night. That night, neither of us acknowledged our feelings for each other. We were back to being the friends we had always been. There are very few people in this solar system I feel comfortable enough to sit and have tea with for an evening. Logi is one of them, and Smooth is the other person. She is just so easy to talk to and such a great listener. You can always tell she is listening because she actually asks questions about the topic I am discussing. Oddly, most people are just stuck in their own minds. Most other people never really dig deeper or try to understand what the other person is saying. They just want to talk about what's important to them.

Logi and I talked about what we were reading and working on in our free time. Logi is very spiritual and was reading a book on the history of yoga. Of course, I was all caught up in the latest Baron Wufot book about his investment philosophy. Both of us are dreamers and I think our choice of books usually supports our personal dreams or visions. In order to become an expert on a subject, it takes a lot of time to learn and read from others. Books usually are the most accessible tool to grow a new knowledge base. I get a sense that Logi is constantly searching for a higher purpose in life, just like me After ninety minutes of yoga and a cup of tea, both of us were relaxed and speaking our minds. Looking back on that night, I can picture it vividly: The table where we were sitting. That we were surrounded by college students who were there studying, and Logi in her neon pink catsuit. For some reason, she didn't even look out of place, she just added to the character of the coffee shop.

Eventually, the lights were dimmed, the signal it was closing time. I offered to call us a taxi, but her dad was already en route to the coffee shop. Her parents had been to a movie and agreed to pick her up on their way home.

I thanked her for another amazing night and for introducing me to the crazy world of disco yoga. She gave me a big hug, then looked directly into my eyes and said she really enjoyed spending time with me and valued my friendship. I was frozen and could barely muster a response. Fortunately, this time I didn't say anything about P/E ratios or personal finance. I squeezed her tight, then we went our own ways.

That evening on the bus ride home, my thoughts were consumed by Logi and becoming her boyfriend. I thought about what it would mean to be her boyfriend. About the fun things we could do, and the places we could travel together. The funny part of the situation, neither of us had really expressed our romantic feelings for each other. In fact, I didn't even know if she felt the same way I did. And if she did feel the same way I did, how was I ever going to get the nerve to get my first kiss? Every time I even thought about kissing Logi, I froze up and got all nervous. It was hilarious and I knew it.

11

Personal Profit and Loss Statement

Baron Wufot'$
Personal Finance Newsletter for Teens
December 1

Net Profit Margin or Savings Rate

Net Profit Margin, also known as Savings Rate, is found by dividing your Profit or Loss by Total Income. For example:

Step 1: Total Income — Total Expenses = Profit or Loss

Step 2: Profit or loss/Total Income = Net Profit Margin (aka Personal Savings Rate)

The Net Profit Margin is important because it shows how well a company performs at converting revenue into profits. A company with a high Net Profit Margin is desirable. A Net Profit Margin over 20% is considered to be high and very desirable for a company.

Value growth investors, like myself, look for stocks that have a Net Profit Margin over 20% and a P/E ratio somewhere between 1x and 20x. Value growth investors like to get a lot for their money, which is why they pick stocks with high Net Profit Margins and low P/E ratios. Who doesn't want to buy a company that is really good at earning high profits and is trading at a discount? This combination can be difficult to find. In order to buy a company at just the right time, it requires a lot of patience and attention.

To invest in value growth stocks, I first compile a watch list of companies from which I would like to buy one day. Then, I patiently wait for the metrics to align. It looks something like this:

	Date	Company	P/E Ratio (target ≤ 20x)	Net Profit Margin (target ≥ 20%)
1.	11/01/19	Doctor and Ramble	23x	27%
2.	11/01/19	Bank of the Universe	28x	19%

3.	11/01/19	Litup Studios	11x	15%
4.	11/01/19	Hulkness Transport	24x	28%
5.	11/01/19	Ultralava Inc.	19x	14%

When a company meets both requirements with a P/E ratio less than 20x and a Net Profit Margin greater than 20%, I think very seriously about investing in the company for the long term.

If there are no companies on my watch list that meet these requirements, then I continue to wait. At the end of each month, I revisit my watch list and update their P/E ratios and Net Profit Margins. This information can easily be found on any major financial website. It may look like this:

Bank of the Universe

Key Ratios

Market Cap	6.2B
Trailing P/E	19.73
Price/Sales	6.03
Price/Book	3.2

Profitability

Net Profit Margin	13.05%
Operating Margin	21.59%

Management Effectiveness

Return on Assets	1.69%
Return on Equity	15.71%

Income Statement
Revenue   1.1B

Often, you may have to wait more than six months before one of your companies meets the criteria of a P/E ratio less than 20x and a Profit Margin greater than 20%.

WHY IS THIS IMPORTANT?

Have you ever heard the saying "buy low, sell high"? By determining when a company is trading low and at a good value, you can time your purchase accordingly. If you buy a good company when it is trading at all-time highs and is overvalued, you will miss your opportunity for earning the better profit margins later. It is better to wait patiently and buy the company at the next dip in the market and then hold it for the rest of your life.

HOW CAN YOU APPLY THIS TO YOUR LIFE AS A TEENAGER?

Here is the fun part. You can calculate Net Profit Margin (aka personal savings rate) for yourself or any individual with an income. It is calculated the exact same way. The only difference is that you are using your own personal net income and net expenses instead of the company's. Let's look at the formula again.

Step 1: Total Income — Total Expenses = Profit or Loss

Step 2: Profit or loss/Total Income = Net Profit Margin, aka Personal Savings Rate

That's right, another word for "savings" is the word "profit." You can use the words interchangeably. I personally like the sound of calculating my monthly "profit" versus "savings." Just my opinion.

Just like looking for companies with a high Net Profit Margin, you should personally aim to have a high Net Profit Margin in your personal life. Sometimes, I like to think of myself as a "Human Corporation" when I am analyzing my personal Net Profit Margin and other financial statistics that can be applied to my life.

Above, I stated that you should look for companies with a Net Profit Margin greater than 20%. For my personal Net Profit Margin, I like to set my goal a lot higher. I try to obtain a monthly Net Profit Margin greater than 50%. Does that sound far-fetched to you? Well, it is very obtainable if you work at it. Here's what the equation would look like.

Total Income for the month of December = $1,000
Total Expenses for the month of December = $500

$1,000 − $500 = $500 profit
$500/$1,000 = 50% Net Profit Margin, aka Personal Savings Rate

ANOTHER ADVANTAGE OF BEING A TEEN

As a teenager, your expenses are going to be a lot lower than almost any adult. As a teen, most likely you don't have to pay a dime for housing, utilities, food, and possibly even transportation. This is a huge advantage and allows teens to save money at extremely high rates. I have seen teenagers obtain a personal Net Profit Margin greater than 80%.

What is your personal Net Profit Margin? Write in and tell me, I would love to hear your successes and struggles.

Now, for the moment you have all been waiting for! Here are the **current standings** for the High School Stock Market Competition!

Update: High School Stock Market Competition—December

	Name	Total	City, State
1.	DivOrDie	$11,007.23	Charlotte, NC
2.	Smootherrific	$10,904.92	St. Louis, MO
3.	SmallCapWonder	$10,756.12	New York, NY
4.	MalibuMadness	$10,723.87	St. Louis, MO
5.	TheBull	$10,717.34	Seattle, WA

Thank you for taking time out of your day to make your life better. You kiddos are what us old people envy. Time is on your side and not mine.

Yours truly,
Baron Wufot

Compounding Interest Fun Fact: If you save $5 per day and invest it in an index fund that yields 7% a year from 16 years old to 65 years old, you will have $760,383 at retirement.

"You guys are killing it!" I shouted as Malibu and Smooth walked into room #244, where we have our monthly Stock Market Club meeting.

"You warned me against penny stocks and said they were the equivalent to gambling on the stock market," Malibu Martin said in excitement with his froggy voice. "Well, look who moved up in the competition. That's right, I'm number four in the whole freaking country. I sold the two worst stocks in my portfolio and bought a couple of penny stocks! One of the penny stocks I purchased sells race car memorabilia and the other penny stock makes tracking devices that can be surgically implanted into humans! Both of their stock prices nearly tripled over the past month. The only thing holding back my virtual portfolio now is the large cap stocks that only returned a couple percent. I am going to continue to dump my large cap stocks to buy more penny stocks. I am going to stomp the comp." Malibu started stomping his right foot and chanting. "I said, stomp the comp. Stomp, stomp the comp. I said, stomp the comp. Stomp, stomp the comp. I said, stomp the comp. Stomp, stomp the comp!"

"Not if I have anything to do with it," Smooth cut in and started chanting. "I'm in second place, you're in fifth. I'm in second place, you're in fifth. I'm in second place, you're in fifth." All the while, Smooth was dancing like a jack-in-the-box. He was cranking one arm while saying, "I'm in second," then exploding out of his imaginary box and shouting, "you're in fifth."

"What is with you guys, acting like cheerleaders! Are you practicing for cheerleading tryouts?" Logi joked as she showed up to the club meeting a little bit late.

"Hahaha, hahaha, you chaps are a riot," Professor Crutchfield said with a big belly laugh. He was sitting in the back of the room correcting papers. "I hope one of you wins it all. If one of you wins it all, I might have to come up with my own victory dance. In all of my years, I have never seen anything like you two chaps."

"I'm just glad you two weirdos are having fun while learning about the stock market. Who would have thought after six weeks you two would be at the top of the competition!" I told them.

"By the way, what do you think DivOrDie means? My guess is it's a reference to a James Bond movie," Smooth surmised. "That person must really know what they are doing to be outperforming my masterly crafted portfolio."

"I think 'Div' stands for dividend. A dividend is a payment some companies make to their shareholders. It is kind of like a gift they give to their investors to thank them for investing in their company," I explained.

"That's cool, do penny stocks give dividends?" Malibu Martin asked.

"Nope, dividends come from the leftover profits. Usually, it is only well-established, large cap stocks that are very profitable that give dividends. Penny stocks usually are not profitable, so they don't have any extra cash to gift in the form of dividends to their investors," I said.

"I'm surprised a dividend-based portfolio would be in first place," Logi added. "Companies that offer dividends are not typically high flying growth stocks that achieve big returns in the short term. I'm guessing that DivOrDie won't be in first place for long if he or she continues to invest in dividend stocks."

"Speaking of profits, was everybody able to put together their own Profit and Loss Statement?" I asked.

"Yap, I cost my parents a whopping $221.51 this past

month!" Smooth bragged. "Of course, that information is confidential. Please keep that within the group, I don't think my parents would be very happy if they knew how much of their money I spent each month."

"You know what they say in the Stock Market Club... 'What happens in the stock market club, stays in the stock market club.' Your profits and losses are safe with us," Malibu Martin joked.

"My lips are sealed," I said. "Now, pass over your personal Profit and Loss Statement, so I can take a look at it."

Smoothelicious's Profit and Loss Statement

November 1st—30th

Income:

Paycheck 1 (Nov 1)	$0
Paycheck 2 (Nov 15)	$0
Total Income	**$0**

Expenses:

Housing or rent	$0
Groceries	$0
Transportation (car pmt, gas, insurance, etc.)	$0
Comic Books	$57.32
Cell phone	$50.74
Pizza	$42.28
Burritos	$31.58
Cheese Puffs	$21.09
Orange Soda	$18.50
Total Expenses	**$221.51**

Total Income − Total Expenses = Profit or Loss
$0.00 − $221.51 = ($221.51) loss

"Smooth, you spent over fifty-seven dollars on comic books last month?" I said in amazement. "How did you manage to get that past your parents?"

"Nice work, guy! Are you taking new students? I would love to learn some of your tricks," Malibu Martin croaked in his froggy voice.

"Some would call it an art! But to be honest with you, this skill of mine was developed for my love of cheese puffs and burritos. Those are powerful forces," joked Smooth.

"I downloaded a compound interest app on my phone, how about we figure out how much your parents' $221.51 would have been worth in 48 years when you retire. That is if you would have saved that money instead of wasting it on your belly," Logi said proudly.

"That's a brilliant idea," I told her. And thought to myself, I'm in love.

"That $221.51 will be worth $6,315 in 48 years, that's assuming the stock market's historical rate of return of 7%," Logi mumbled in disbelief. "So basically, Smooth, you just ate $6,000 worth of pizza and burritos in one month!"

"I knew I could eat, but that is next level. I should enter that hot dog eating contest they have in New York every year," Smooth beamed.

"Smooth, I think the point Logi is trying to make is that our money is worth a lot more in the future, especially if we start saving it now. Maybe, you should continue to swindle your parents out of $200 a month and invest it in the stock market!" I joked.

"That's a great idea. You know, if you were able to obtain and contribute $200 a month from your parents and invested it in the stock market, that would come to $943,183 at retirement. Smooth, you could continue to eat cheese puffs for the rest of your life or you could become a millionaire. The choice is all yours, big boy," Logi told him.

"You mean to tell me my belly will consume nearly a million dollars worth of junk food by retirement. That's actually kind of disgusting," Smooth muttered.

"Okay, I'll go next," Malibu Martin piped up. "I took in $300 for doing my chores this month. My chores consisted of mowing the lawn a couple of times, doing the nightly dinner dishes, walking the pup, and throwing out the trash. Of that, I spent $215 and saved $85. I'm hoping to save up enough money for another Hucci rucksack!"

"More like a schmuck sack," Smooth poked.

"Dude, nobody gives you crap about your style," Malibu Martin barked back.

Malibu had a good point. Smooth was wearing his usual outfit, an old pair of purple and yellow basketball shoes, a Hawaiian flower print shirt with hula girls on it, and cargo shorts. I had to agree with Malibu Martin on this one, Smooth shouldn't be making fun of anybody's style. There's no way I would be caught in Smooth's digs (aka, clothes).

"Alright, Malibu, let's see your personal Profit and Loss Statement for the month of November, pass it on over," I asked.

"Here's the quick and dirty version. It's nothing fancy," Malibu told us.

Malibu BuBaby's P&L Statement
November 1st—30th

Income:	$300
Expenses:	
Girls	$82.57
GetLit Coffee Shop	$54.12
Gasoline	$50.56
Gottagetta Burger	$27.75
Cell phone	$0
Total Expenses	**$215.00**

Total Income − Total Expenses = Profit or Loss
$300 − $215 = $85.00 Profit

"Not bad, Malibu Madness. You and Smooth need to talk to my parents about my funds. I'm not getting a cent out of them," I joked. "Now for the fun part. Lovely Logi Laru, what does that come to if Malibu saves $85 a month until retirement?"

"Well at 7% rate of return, which is the historical market average, Malibu would have roughly $400,852 saved up at the age of 64," Logi answered.

"That's amazing, I have never even thought about having that much money ever, like in the history of the universe. You mean to tell me I can save $400,000 just by contributing $85 a month to an investment account that is invested in an index fund? That's rad, just think how many Hucci rucksacks I can buy with $400,000!" Malibu Martin said in amazement.

"Why aren't we all saving as much money as possible right now?" Smooth asked. I'm going to have to rethink my burritos and cheese puff habits. Franklin, can you help me land a sweet job like yours?

"It would be my pleasure, but only if you give me some insight into your investment strategies," I kidded Smootherific.

"All right, I think it is your turn, champ, to show us your Profit and Loss Statement. Or should we just call it your Profit Machine Statement?" joked Malibu Martin.

"I like that, my Profit Machine Statement because I don't really plan on losing money any time soon," I said as I started passing out my Profit Statement. As I did so, though, I was starting to get a little nervous. This was the first time I had ever shared my financials with anyone.

Franklin Fi's Personal Profit and Loss Statement

November 1st—30th

Income:

Paycheck 1 (Nov 1)	$112.32
Paycheck 2 (Nov 15)	$280.87
Total Income	**$393.19**

Expenses:

Housing	$0
Utilities	$0
Groceries	$0
Lunch Money	$62.78
Phone	$32.28
Bike Tires	$28.34
Entertainment	$27.87
Other Transportation	$15.85
Total Expenses	**$167.12**

Total Income − Total Expenses = Profit or Loss
$393.19 − $167.12 = $226.07 PROFIT!!!

"And the best part, I was able to open my first brokerage savings account and make my first investment. I'm in the game!" I shouted. "I thought I would never start saving, but once you get a job it becomes easy. You have less time to spend money because all of your free time is now spent working. The first pay period I worked twelve hours because I was training. The second pay period I worked weekends, so I worked a total of four days the second paycheck. Going forward, I am going to start working a couple of weekdays after school."

"You should invest in comic books!" Smooth cut in, but I kept talking.

"Once I got my first paycheck, I begged my dad to cosign on a brokerage investment account. To my surprise, he loved the idea. I'm in the game!!!" I told them.

"Dude, you are a madman. Why didn't you tell us you opened an account?" Malibu questioned me. "That's so freaking awesome, like in all caps. A-W-E-S-O-M-E. Let me know if you need any tips on penny stocks, they're hot. I bet we can turn that $226 into over $2gees, as in 2 grand, as in $2k, as in $2,000 big ones. We can't miss with penny stocks. They're hot, H-O-T!"

Of course, I didn't have the heart to tell Malibu Martin I wasn't interested in his penny stocks. But, he was in fourth place in the stock market competition, so who was I to give him investment advice? My actual plan was to build a watch list of twenty companies and wait until one of them hit the magic numbers of a Net Profit Margin greater than 20%

and a P/E ratio around 12x to 15x. In addition, I was using my virtual stock market account from the competition to learn how certain individual stocks traded up and down throughout each month. I made sure to buy value growth stocks at a good price that I could hold for possibly the rest of my life. But before I invested in any individual stocks, I put over half of my savings, or about $125, into an S&P 500 index fund. With half of my money, I plan to invest in individual stocks and the other half in an index fund. I wanted to ensure to follow Baron Wufot's advice to invest in an index fund every month to capture the historical market rate of return of 7%.

"For the fun part, let's look at how much you will have once compounding interest goes to work for you," Logi said with enthusiasm. "The $226.07 you managed to save last month and invest will be worth $6,445.15 at retirement! That's without making any other contributions. That's crazy. You can turn $226 into $6,445 just by investing it in a conservative index fund and letting it compound over a long period of time!"

"Logi, what are you entering into your compounding interest app or calculator to get these crazy numbers?" Smooth asked.

"Here, I'll walk you through it. Here are the data fields my compounding interest app asks for and how I fill them in:

Compound Interest Calculator

Current Investment Amount:	$226.07
Annual Rate of Return:	7%
Investment Length:	48 years
Monthly Contribution:	$0

Answer: You invested **$226.07** in a fund that yields **7%** a year. If you contribute an additional **$0 Monthly** for **48 years**, that fund will be worth

$6,445.15

That is **$226.07** of your contribution and **$6,219.15 profit**

"That's super interesting. So compounding interest is basically working out the interest for the first year, adding it to the total, then calculating the interest for the next period, adding it to the total, and so on. Or another way to think of it is 'interest on interest.' The longer the period of time, the more time your interest has to compound at greater amounts," Malibu stated. "Like this!"

Year 1	$1,000 × 10% = $100	$1,000 + $100 = $1,100
Year 2	$1,100 × 10% = $110	$1,100 + $110 = $1,210
Year 3	$1,210 × 10% = $121	$1,210 + $121 = $1,331

"Or, in the case of my savings, here's a shortcut if you want to add a percentage to a number: you multiply the number ($226.07) by **1 plus the percentage fraction** (7% is equal to 0.07). For example," I showed them.

Year 1	$226.07 × 1.07 = $242.41
Year 2	$242.41 × 1.07 = $259.94
Year 3	$259.94 × 1.07 = $278.73
Year 4	etc.... All the way to year 48
Year 47	$5,605.42 × 1.07 = $6,010.64
Year 48	$6,010.64 × 1.07 = $6,445.15

"Wowzers! That is insane how fast your money compounds in the later years," Logi Laru exclaimed. "The first year you are only getting 7% of the initial deposit of $226.07, which only comes to $16.34. Then in year 47, you are getting the same 7% return, just on a larger amount due to compounding interest. You are actually earning 7% of $5,605.42, which comes to a profit of $405.22 for doing absolutely nothing. That amount is almost double your initial investment of $226.07. Do you understand now why it is so important to invest long-term as a teenager? It is very possible you only have to spend ten or fifteen years of your life working full time. Then the rest of the years you can just let your money work for you."

"Okay, now can you plug in a contribution of $226.07 a month for 48 years? Remember, this is totally hypothetical because that number might be less or a lot more depending on where I am in my career. Anybody have any guesses before Logi enters the **$226.07 monthly contribution** into her compounding interest app?" I asked them.

"Like $2 billion," joked Smooth. "My mind is still blown away that you can turn $226.07 into like $7,000 by doing nothing. Isn't that somehow illegal?"

"You are way off, Smooth. And no, it is not illegal. It just takes being a little smarter than everybody else and a lot of patience to let your investment compound over the years," Logi said.

"I'm going with $800,000," Martin guessed.

"That's a little more realistic, but no, still wrong," Logi answered. "Franklin, what's your guess?"

"Logi, how long have you known me? Don't you know me better than that? That's the first thing I did when I deposited my paychecks. I had to know how much money I could potentially be worth at retirement, so I did the math. If I contribute $226.07 every month for the rest of my career, I will have a cool $1,072,572.53 at retirement. Yes, that's right! I am on track to be worth a million big ones, just by working at Paddle Department Store. I wouldn't even have to switch jobs, increase my hours, or even get a pay raise to become a millionaire. It's freakin' unbelievable!" I shouted out of excitement.

"You chaps are getting a little out of control today. What's all of the commotion about?" Professor Crutchfield asked us, as he looked up from a stack of papers he was grading.

"Oh, nothing, sir. Just that Franklin Fi decided to inform us he is worth over a million dollars," Smooth bragged.

"He's what?! I know his parents. For that matter, I know all of your parents and I have a hard time believing any of you kids have seen that kind of money in your life. Franklin, how did you manage to get a million dollars?" Professor Crutchfield asked.

"Sir, I think Smooth is pulling a smooth move. I just showed the club how I made $226.07 this past month and put it in a brokerage savings account. Then Logi calculated, if I contribute that same $226.07 for the rest of my career until retirement, it'll compound to over a million dollars," I clarified.

"Look, Professor Crutchfield," Logi said and showed him how the compounding interest app worked on her phone.

Compound Interest Calculator

Current Investment Amount:	$226.07
Annual Rate of Return:	7%
Investment Length:	48 years
Monthly Contribution:	$226.07

Answer: You invested **$226.07** in a fund that yields 7% a year. If you contribute an additional **$226.07 monthly** for **48 years**, that fund will be worth **$1,072,572.53**

That is **$130,442.39** of your contribution
and **$942,130.14 profit**

"Can you believe that, Professor Crutchfield? Franklin Fi is on his way to becoming a millionaire," Malibu Martin said excitedly. "The best part is how you can turn $226 a month into a million bucks. It works out he will only have to contribute a total of $130,442 over the next 48 years and in return he gets $942,130 for doing nothing except being smart enough to invest $226 a month. Shoot! My mom tells me all the time that it costs $300,000 to raise a kid. The way I spend my parents' money, I probably cost more like $500,000. Maybe I should convince my parents to start an investment fund for me!"

"Hahahahahaha!!!" You chaps are a riot. "Yes, Franklin's got a good start but it is going to take a lot of hard work and a lot of saving to get there. There's no doubt in my mind that Franklin or any of you for that matter can become that wealthy, if you put your mind to it," Professor Crutchfield proudly told us. "In fact, I have been teaching and saving for the last forty years and I am living proof that compound interest really works. I was fortunate enough to have learned the power of compounding interest from my old mentor. At the time, I was a fresh-faced twenty-four-year-old and had just started teaching. My mentor, Remmy Butler, was just about ready to retire from teaching. He took me aside one day and explained his retirement plan to me. He shared that he had used the power of compound interest to amass a small fortune. Ever since, I have been saving a large portion of my teaching salary and investing it in the stock market. Hopefully, next year I will retire. I plan on spending the rest of my life traveling the world. And I have worked hard for it!"

"Wow, that is really cool, sir. You are living proof that compounding interest actually works," I stated. "It is one thing to hear it from the mysterious Baron Wufot, the richest man in the solar system, but to hear it from you makes it real. It is awesome to hear that even as a teacher if you play your cards right you can retire wealthy. Without being too nosey, is there anything further you can share with us?"

"Yes, there is one term I would like to share with you chaps. I haven't heard the term 'dollar cost averaging' mentioned at any of these club meetings. Dollar cost averaging is the concept of buying a particular investment at a fixed dollar amount, on a regular schedule no matter the share price. For me, I purchased the same dollar amount of an S&P 500 index fund on the same day of every month for the last forty years. This concept is known as dollar cost averaging. If you apply this concept over a long period of time, you will end up buying it when it is trading at both highs and lows. As a result, over time the cost per share averages out. This is a great way you can lower the risk in a given investment," Professor Crutchfield explained.

"That sounds like an interesting concept. I will definitely look further into dollar cost averaging. It makes sense, especially considering we have a lot of years to invest in front of us," I told Professor Crutchfield.

"Son, it's all about reducing risk and maximizing your profits. The ideal situation is when you get to the point your investment portfolio is on autopilot. I'll never forget reading that 80% of stock pickers don't beat the market average. I don't like those odds, so I figured early I would rather invest in an index fund that mirrors the overall market and not have to worry about outperforming the professionals. My philosophy worked for me, but it is important to educate yourself and find a strategy that works for you," Professor Crutchfield said.

Investment Tip:

Dollar cost averaging refers to the process of buying (irrespective of share price) a fixed dollar amount of a particular investment on a periodic, regular schedule. Because the dollar amount does not change, the result is fewer shares being purchased when prices are high and more shares purchased when prices are low. Over time, the cost per share tends to average out. Through this process, an investor reduces his or her risk of investing a large amount in a single investment at the wrong time.

"Dude, I got to get a job like yesterday," joked Smooth.

"Yeah, me too!" Malibu ribbitted. "You know how many Hucci rucksacks I can buy for a million dollars? I don't know either, but it's a lot. You might even be able to buy the whole company. That's rad!"

"Yeah, we're not talking about buying cheese puffs anymore. You are next level brohammity sandwich," Smooth said in disbelief.

"Calm down! I have saved over $226 in the past month.

That is a long way from a million dollars. I still have to work another forty-seven years and eleven months to get there. Another way to look at it is that I am worth 15% of one $1,500 Hucci rucksack, which is a long way from owning the factory. Although, it is nice to know I have Professor Crutchfield here to help guide me through at least the next couple of years," I told the group.

"Franklin, this is really cool. Just look at you, bubba," Smooth started in. "Last meeting you were saying how much you wanted to get a job. Now you have a job and you have started your grand adventure down the yellow brick road. Well, Dorothy, you are on your way. I kind of feel like your scarecrow. I'm proud of you, man."

"Ain't that the truth, but with half the brains as the scarecrow," joked Malibu Martin.

"Dude, cut me some slack. I will be the first to admit I say some dumb stuff sometimes, but you've got to admit, I at least have as many brains as the scarecrow," Smooth said and he was dead serious.

"You guys are ridiculous. The scarecrow didn't have any brains. Have you even seen the movie?" Logi cut them off.

"You guys fight like a married couple," I told them. "In all honesty, I'm really glad to have these club meetings to help keep me motivated. Okay, enough about me, Logi you're up. Are you ready to present your personal Profit and Loss Statement?"

"You know it! But I have never really shared this information with anyone outside of my family," Logi said with a little doubt in her voice. "Please don't share this information with anybody else and please don't think any differently of me. This is kind of tough for me."

"You know what they say about the Stock Market Club.

'What happens in the stock market club, stays in the stock market club.' I promise to keep this info in-house," Smooth reassured Logi.

I didn't really know what to expect. I knew that Logi's parents were both doctors and had been putting money aside for her in a 529 College Savings Plan, which is some sort of a tax-free savings account for college. But I was not prepared at all for the bomb that Logi was about to drop on us...

She went on to tell us she was a trillionaire and the heir to the throne in India. No, not really! But she still blew me away with what she was about to tell us.

Logi Laru's Profit and Loss Statement

November 1st—30th

Income:

529 College Savings Plan	$1,000
Dowry Savings	$2,000
Tutoring	$300
Total Income	**$3,300**

Expenses:

Housing	$0
Transportation	$0
Phone	$0
Yoga Classes	$78.53
Food and Entertainment	$60.01
Books	$48.37
Art Supplies	$22.95
Total Expenses	**$209.86**

Total Income − Total Expenses = Profit or Loss
$3,300 − $209.86 = $3,090.14 Profit

Logi passed out her Profit and Loss Statement and my heart exploded. What the heck is a dowry deposit for $2,000 doing on there? Isn't that what you pay the groom's family in India for him to marry your daughter? Is she expected to marry someone else or is she already promised to somebody else? Is it even India where they arrange marriages? At what age does that happen? How foolish of me to think I had a chance with Logi Laru. She's probably promised to the Prince of India.

"Logi, you are loaded, like a baked potato!" Malibu croaked in his frog-like voice. "Wanna go on a date this weekend? Nah, just joking. Do you, though? Why didn't you ever tell us how much coin you had stashed? And why in the world do you wear the same blue jeans and gray shirt to school every day, if you have so much money? And why, why do you ride that old bike to school when you could have any car you wanted. I'm perplexed, you must be worth six figures."

Logi embarrassingly said, "Please, Martin, I wasn't sure if I should share this information with the club. I really don't want anybody to look at me differently and please don't share this with anybody outside of the club."

"I'm just peanut butter and jealous," joked Smooth.

"Smooth, that is hilarious! Peanut butter and jealous," Malibu said while laughing.

"You shouldn't be embarrassed your parents want you to succeed. That's really cool they have been preparing for you to go to college," I said without trying to sound disappointed about her dowry.

BUT THE DOWRY!!! I screamed inside my head. How can I ever look at her the same way? She's untouchable. I will never even have a chance to love her. This isn't fair. I quit! This is so ridiculous. My mind was about to explode.

"So your parents give you $2,000 every month for writing in your diary? What kind of diary is it that you get that much money for? Is it some sort of a bibliography you are writing?" Smooth asked unknowingly.

"Smooth, it's a dowry, not a diary. I think you also meant to say autobiography, not bibliography. Sorry, I didn't mean to correct you. Sometimes it just comes out. Smooth, a dowry is a sum of money the bride's parents in India give to the groom's family when they get married. It is an Indian tradition that dates back hundreds, if not thousands of years," Logi informed us.

"So some Indian dude is going to get bucket loads of money to marry you?" Malibu Martin prodded. "But you're like beautiful and could have any guy at St. Louis High!"

"My parents are old-fashioned and they have it in their heads I am going to marry someone from their home country and then have a big Indian wedding," Logi told us.

I couldn't believe what I was hearing. My mouth didn't move, it was frozen shut. My heart was shattered, I was devastated. My plans for a life and kids with Logi were dismantled in a matter of minutes. I hadn't even got to kiss her yet. How could I have been so stupid? Is life really that fragile, that unpredictable? In a matter of minutes, my life had imploded. When I was presenting my Profit and Loss Statement, I was the happiest kid in the school, then BOOM! Everything was blown apart.

Brrrrriiiiinnnngggggg!!! Brrrrriiiiinnnngggggg!!!
Brrrrriiiiinnnngggggg!!!

The bell rang and I rushed out of the classroom trying not to look heartbroken. Although, I didn't do a very good job at it. I just couldn't look at her and the rest of the gang. I was so embarrassed. I just ran out of there as fast as I could.

12

Breakup

The next month, I pretty much hung out with Smooth and Malibu. If I wasn't with those guys, then I was at work at Paddle Store or at the library reading books on the stock market. I was dead set on increasing my personal savings rate. At the library, I read every book I could find on frugality.

Later that month, I wrote Baron Wufot a letter informing him of my commitment to saving and I even included a copy of my personal Profit and Loss Statement, along with Savings Rate. The Baron had asked his readers to write in and share their personal savings rate and to tell him how they were doing it. I wasn't about to pass up the opportunity to tell him about my journey into the workforce. If he wanted us to write to him, you better believe I was going to jump on the opportunity. Even if he really didn't read my letter.

Dear Mr. Wufot,

I don't know if you remember me, but my name is Franklin Fi. I helped you create the High School Stock Market Competition. Thank you for sponsoring the competition. It's going great, I'm somewhere in the middle of the pack with my value stocks. You know, the ones you like so much. It's been a great experience so far and I am learning a lot. Early on in the competition, I decided I would not alter my investment style to try and win such a short competition. Instead, I decided it was better to learn how my own strategy worked when I put it use. The competition has been a perfect training ground for my personal portfolio. You inspired me to get my first job and to open my first brokerage savings account. I even put a little money into an index fund, just like you suggested. Don't get me wrong, I would love to win the $10,000 prize! I just can't justify gambling on the stock market. Odds are I would lose badly, and even worse not learn anything from the whole experience.

You asked your readers to write and tell you about their own personal savings rates. I am excited to inform you that your list of potential jobs really helped me land my first job a little over a month ago. With a little ingenuity, I was fortunate to become gainfully employed at Paddle Department Store. The first month I made $393.19 after taxes. Of that, I spent $167.12, which means I saved $226.07 for the month of November. This makes my Savings Rate or Net Profit Margin a whopping 57.5%. I set my goal of 60% for the month of December. Although, I have a feeling that may be hard to achieve because I have a big family and have to buy Christmas presents for everyone. Below, I have provided you with my personal Savings Rate calculation. You are right, it is really easy to save as a teenager because we don't have to pay for housing, transportation, utilities, and food. I plan on saving as much money as possible in my teenage years.

Total Income − Total Expenses = Profit or Loss
$393.19 − $167.12 = **$226.07 PROFIT!!!**

Personal Savings Rate (Net Profit Margin)
Profit ÷ Total Income = Personal Savings Rate
$226.07 ÷ $393.19 = **57.5%**

Compounding Interest
If I invested my profit of $226.07 in a fund that yields 7% a year and I don't contribute any additional money for 48 years, that fund will be worth $6,445.15. **That means if I invest $226.07 today, at retirement it will be worth $6,445.15 for a profit of $6,219.08!**

But I'm not done yet. My goal is not to only contribute that $226.07 just one time. I plan on contributing $226.07 every month until retirement in **48 years**. If I invested **$226.07** in the stock market that historically yields **7%** a year and contribute an additional **$226.07 monthly** for **48 years**, I will have at retirement **$1,072,572.53!**

Some people call me a dreamer, but I think this is very doable. I am off to a good start. With the added motivation and guidance I get from your newsletter, I have a great chance of staying on track.

Thank you for taking the time to help me and my generation. You are the best!

Sincerely,
Franklin Fi
St. Louis High School

Smooth was especially cool and supportive during the month of December. I think he could tell how heartbroken I was over Logi.

Smooth even mentioned that he felt somewhat responsible for the whole situation. You see, Smooth and Malibu Martin had actually plotted to hook up Logi and me. They sensed we both liked each other but figured neither of us had the nerve to ask the other on a date. When Logi asked if anybody wanted to go to the City Museum with her, it was the perfect opportunity to execute their plan. Smooth never went to his cousin's bar mitzvah. His cousin doesn't even exist and I fell for it. Malibu did, in fact, have tickets to the Justin Sleeper concert, making it convenient for Malibu Martin to say no. I totally would have gone to the Justin Sleeper concert as well.

They thought their plan worked when they saw us falling in love. Then the dowry.... They had no idea about Logi's dowry and were thrown the same curveball as I had.

I should have known! Any plan that Smooth was behind was bound to go wrong. We don't call him Smooth because he's smooth. In reality, he is the exact opposite of smooth. He's my best friend but I have come to accept his shortfalls as I smooth on. He doesn't mean any harm to anybody, he's just being himself. More times than not, his plans don't work out as planned. Smooth was just trying to be a good wingman. I had feelings for Logi long before they came up with the idea to get us together. They were just trying to do me a favor. That's what friends are for!

One good thing that came from it was I started hanging out every weekend night with Smooth and Malibu. One weekend, we caught a St. Louis Blues hockey game. The next weekend, we went to a concert down at the landing on the Mississippi River. Another night, we went to a St. Louis University basketball game. That month was a blast and they really helped me get over Logi. That's what friends do for each other.

I was told once to make friends with people who want what's best for you. There's no doubt in my mind these two have my back. Smooth and Malibu definitely care for me and I couldn't ask for better friends.

Eventually, I came to the realization that Logi and I were always just friends. We were never boyfriend and girlfriend. I got caught up in my emotions and developed strong feelings for her, which she did not share. It was all in my head. By the end of the month, I decided to let it go and focus on just being a teenager. With good friends like Smooth and Malibu, it was a lot easier.

13

Index Funds for Life

Baron Wufot's
Personal Finance Newsletter for Teens
January 2

Stocks, Bonds, Mutual Funds, Index Funds. What does it all mean?

As a teenager, you have a long time to let your money grow and compound. By investing while in your teens, you have more than forty years for your money to compound until retirement. Time and compounding interest are your most powerful tools.

The stock market goes up, down, sideways, and diagonal. Nobody on the planet can predict how it will perform. It really is difficult to accurately predict what is going to happen next. As an individual investor with a long investment time frame, you don't have to worry about any of these moves because the stock market has historically moved upward on average of 7% a year. The S&P 500 index has historically averaged returns of around 7% since 1928. That is ninety years of data! If you just look at the last fifteen years, you'll see an average return of over 11%.

S&P 500 Annual Returns (15 years)

Dec. 31, 2018	10.56%
Dec. 31, 2017	21.83%
Dec. 31, 2016	11.96%
Dec. 31, 2015	1.38%
Dec. 31, 2014	13.69%
Dec. 31, 2013	32.39%
Dec. 31, 2012	16.00%
Dec. 31, 2011	2.11%
Dec. 31, 2010	15.06%
Dec. 31, 2009	26.46%
Dec. 31, 2008	−37.00%
Dec. 31, 2007	5.49%
Dec. 31, 2006	15.79%
Dec. 31, 2005	4.91%
Dec. 31, 2004	10.88%
Dec. 31, 2003	28.68%
Average	**11.26%**

As an individual investor, you need to get into the game as soon as possible. Time is on your side when you are young. Don't worry about where the market is trading, worry about getting a job and putting your hard-earned money to work for as long as possible.

NOW THAT YOU HAVE A JOB AND HAVE MADE A LITTLE MONEY, WHERE SHOULD YOU PARK YOUR MONEY FOR THE NEXT FORTY YEARS?

The quick and easy answer is to invest your money into an **Index Fund** by using a concept called **Dollar Cost Averaging (DCA)**.

What is Dollar Cost Averaging?

Dollar cost averaging refers to the process of buying (irrespective of share price) a fixed dollar amount of a particular investment on a periodic, regular schedule. Because the dollar amount does not change, the result is fewer shares being purchased when prices are high and more shares purchased when prices are low. Over time, the cost per share tends to average out. Through this process, an investor reduces his or her risk of investing a large amount in a single investment at the wrong time.

What is an Index Fund?

An index fund is a type of mutual fund with a portfolio constructed to match or track the components of a market index, such as the Standard & Poor's 500 index (S&P 500). An index mutual fund is said to provide broad market exposure, low operating expenses, and low portfolio turnover.

In other words, an index fund is an investment tool that mirrors a stock market index. For example, the SPDR S&P 500 ETF (the ticker is

SPY) is an index fund that mirrors the S&P 500 index. The idea is that if the S&P 500 trades up 7%, then so will the SPY index fund. SPY trades just like an individual stock or company. You can buy shares in SPY through almost any brokerage account. If SPY is not the best index fund for you, there are many others, for example, VTSAX, IJR, VOO, and VEA, just to name a few.

I am not here to tell you exactly where to put your money, that is up to you. I am simply suggesting that investing in an index fund is a low-risk way to outperform roughly 80% of the investors in the game. You can eliminate a lot of the work and still harness the power of compounding interest by investing in index funds.

I think it is important for you to learn about the other investment tools that are available to you. The most common investment tools are stocks, bonds, and mutual funds. The following are the definitions for each term. You may do additional research on your own if you choose.

What is a Stock?

A stock (also known as "shares" and "equity") is a type of security that signifies ownership in a corporation and represents a claim on part of the corporation's assets and earnings.

What is a Bond?

A bond is a fixed income investment in which an investor loans money to an entity (typically corporate or governmental) that borrows the funds for a defined period of time at a variable or fixed interest rate. Bonds are used by companies, municipalities, states, and sovereign governments to raise money and finance a variety of projects and activities. Owners of bonds are debtholders, or creditors, of the issuer.

What is a Mutual Fund?

A mutual fund is an investment vehicle made up of a pool of money collected from many investors for the purpose of investing in securities such as stocks, bonds, money market instruments, and other assets. Mutual funds are operated by professional money managers, who allocate the fund's investments and attempt to produce capital gains and/or income for the fund's investors. A mutual fund's portfolio is structured and maintained to match the investment objectives stated in its prospectus.

WHAT TYPE OF INVESTOR ARE YOU?

To help you understand your investment options. I have put together a summary below to help you choose what type of investment you may want to make.

Risk and Reward for Each Investment

Stocks
Upside: Stocks can offer the highest return on your investment.
Downside: The possibility of high returns comes higher risk and a larger downside.

Index Funds
Upside: Medium to high returns, very low management fees. A cheap and low-risk way to benefit from the market.
Downside: Limited downside if invested over a long period of time. Investing in an index fund over a short period of time can carry risk, as in any short-term speculation.

Bonds
Upside: Medium returns
Downside: Medium risk, missed opportunities to grow your wealth

Mutual Funds
Upside: Medium to high returns
Downside: High management fees that can eat into your returns, mutual funds can charge investors thousands of dollars a year.

The most important thing for you as a teenager is to start saving! Once you have started to save, find an investment vehicle to put your money into and leave your money there for as long as possible. Time and compounding interest will make you a lot more money than trying to be a good stock picker. If I was sixteen years old and just starting out again, I would park the majority of my savings into an index fund and then learn to invest in stocks with 5-10% of my savings.

Bonds serve a purpose, but they are better investment tools closer to the age of retirement when you are working to preserve your savings, not grow it. Mutual funds can be expensive and I don't see the reason to invest in them when you can invest in an index fund.

Now, for the moment you have all been waiting for! Here are the **current standings** for the High School Stock Market Competition!

Update: High School Stock Market Competition—January

	Name	Total	City, State
1.	Smootherrific	$11,995.23	St. Louis, MO
2.	MalibuMadness	$11,704.92	St. Louis, MO
3.	ImShortButImLong	$11,456.12	New York, NY
4.	TheBull	$11,223.87	Seattle, WA
5.	SmallCapWonder	$11,117.34	New York, NY

Thank you for taking time out of your day to make your life better. You kiddos are who us old people envy. Time is on your side and not mine.

Happy New Year!
Baron Wufot

Compounding Interest Fun Fact: If you invest $1 a day into an S&P 500 index fund, it will take 76 years for that fund to be worth over a million dollars. If you invest $5 a day in that same fund, it will take 53 years for that fund to be worth over a million dollars. There is no excuse not to start saving immediately, if you are fit and able.

Group Text: StL Stock Market Club

Smooth: Malibu, you suck! Have you seen the latest Baron Wufot newsletter? I'm in first place and you are in second place. If you're not in first, then you might as well be in last.

Malibu: Dude, I'm closing in on you. You bought some penny stocks, didn't you?

Franklin Fi: You guys are making me look bad. STOP!

Smooth: Penny stocks are where it's at! I'm buying more this month. As fast, as fast can be, you'll never catch me.

Logi: Slow and steady. You boys make sure you are learning something from this competition.

Smooth: I'm learning how to win $10,000 big ones.

Franklin Fi: We are about halfway there. You're playing with fire if you keep buying penny stocks. Dude, you should look into something a little more conservative to preserve your lead.

Smooth: What are you talking about. I'm going to stay on offense. I ain't scurred.

Franklin Fi: Happy Hanukkah, your Smoothness.

Malibu: Yeah, merry Xmas to all! Let's get together over the break.

Logi: Let's do it! How about at Litup Coffee? Tomorrow?

Smooth: I'm in. How about 2 pm?

Franklin Fi: Sorry, can't this week. I picked up some extra hours at work. Double time, baby!

Logi: Okay, we'll miss you. Smooth and Malibu, I'll see you tomorrow!

14

Teens on Coffee

"Hey, guys!" Logi said as she sat down. "Sorry, I'm running a little bit late. It's cold out there, which makes for slow going on a bicycle."

"It's all good," Smooth responded. "Malibu and I were just talking about what penny stocks we should buy next."

"We're going to run away with this competition," Malibu bragged. "Our penny stocks are up 50% since the competition started. We're going to dump all of our other stocks and only invest in penny stocks."

"If you guys were smart, you would play a little defense and put some of your money into an index fund," Logi advised them. "You already have a big enough lead to win it all."

"What fun would that be," Smooth exclaimed. "Besides, I still have to hold off Malibu."

"You two! I'm glad you guys have chosen to bond over the stock market," Logi told them.

"Speaking of getting along. Are you and Franklin getting along?" Malibu Martin asked Logi.

"Dude, not cool," Smooth said as he kicked Malibu Martin under the table.

"It's alright, I was wanting to talk to you guys about that anyway. It's probably best that Franklin couldn't make it today," Logi continued. "Do you think he's mad at me because my parents have been helping me save for college? He works a lot of hours, and I totally understand how he could resent me."

"I don't think that is exactly the problem," Smooth said.

"Really? What's his deal then?" Logi questioned.

"I think you hurt his feelings, because…he…kind of…just a little bit…un poco…like a happy meal size…a smidgeon…," Smooth stuttered.

"Lord almighty, just say it already," Malibu Martin cut in.

"Franklin likes you! He thinks you are the suppenkuchen, the shiznit," Smooth blurted out. "I don't know how else to say it. He likes you like spicy green curry!"

"Like spicy green curry? What is that supposed to mean?" Logi questioned.

"I don't know how else to say it. He has a drunken noodle over you," Smooth continued to mix up words and make a fool out of himself. "You're his supreme pizza, the monster burger, a croque monsieur!"

"He likes me like a ham and cheese sandwich?" Logi asked as she turned bright red.

"Bro-ham sandwich, I think she gets the point," Malibu cut in. "In short, when he found out you had a dowry, you broke his heart. Franklin thinks you have already been promised to some prince in India and he doesn't have a chance with you."

"That's not how it even works!" Logi shouted and stood up

to walk out. "I'm a sixteen-year-old girl and I am not an object to win or to be given away. Do you guys really think that? You freaking jerks, that's my culture. That's how my parents were raised and their parents before them!"

"Honestly, I didn't even know what a diary was before last month. Sheesh!" Smooth protested.

Logi shoved her chair into the table and ran out of the coffee shop, crying.

"Why can't I ever say or do anything right?" Smooth said as he tipped up his coffee cup and attempted to drink it all in one big gulp. "Ahhwee, mother of St. Harry… my freaking tongue, that's hot, hot, H-O-T! My tongue is inflamed, it's inflamed!!!"

"You're a maniac!" Malibu Martin said as he pounded on the table. "You're out of your gourd, dude."

"My tongue is inflamed, it's inflamed!!!" Smooth continued to yell out in pain.

That night just before going to bed, I got a phone call from Malibu and he relived the whole Smooth and Logi conversation for me. I couldn't believe it. For someone who can't get his words straight, Smooth has quite a large vocabulary.

"What was Smooth thinking! He seriously said, 'Franklin likes you like spicy green curry?' What does that even mean? I've had red curry and it's alright but never green curry. What was he thinking! No one in the history of the universe has ever said something so ridiculous. I like her like spicy green curry?! I'm going to body-slam Smooth the next time I see him!" I shouted into the telephone at Malibu Martin.

"Oh, my favorite part was when he said you had a drunken noodle for her. How's it even possible to confuse a dish from Thailand with liking a girl? Where does he come up with this stuff?" Malibu said while laughing.

"Did you say he was drinking coffee? I thought he was banned from drinking coffee. He just gets too worked up. Smooth is such an animal sometimes, he just reacts and forgets to think about the repercussions to what he is saying. Now I really don't have a chance with Logi," I told Malibu.

"Yeah, he had coffee. You should have seen him when he tried to drink the last half of his coffee in one gulp. You know that dance he does, the one we call the 'Smooth Dance' where he pumps his hands up and down and shakes his belly? He was doing the Smooth Dance while screaming 'Hot! Hot! H-O-T, I'm inflamed, my tongue is inflamed!" Malibu said while laughing so hard that he was crying.

"Stop it, Bu, you are giving me a drunken noodle, I can't take any more of this!" I told Malibu Martin.

"This is Sam Smooth," Smooth said as he answered his cell phone

"What were you thinking!" I said while trying to not completely lose it on Smooth.

"Dude, I am so sorry," Smooth apologized. "I didn't know what to say and I panicked. You know how I get when I drink coffee. I totally blacked out. The last thing I remember is Logi asking why you had been avoiding her over Christmas break. Oh, I screwed up Franklin. I'm sorry. I spilled the beans, all of them. You name a bean and I spilled it. I spilled the coffee beans, the garbanzo beans, the string beans, the jelly beans, the kidney beans, you name it and I spilled it today. I feel horrible, I was just trying to help a brother out."

"Just to be clear, at some point you did tell her that I like her?" I asked.

"Dude, yes I told her that you like her. How did you miss that part?" Smooth said.

"Then you somehow came up with the idea that I liked her like spicy green curry and that I have a drunken noodle for her?" I questioned furiously.

"I am so sorry, man. I know how much you like her and I was just trying to hook up my best friend with the girl of his dreams," Smooth mumbled into the phone.

"Smooth, I have a drunken noodle for you right now," I said in disbelief.

"I screwed up, I know. Franklin, please don't be mad at me. Let me call Logi and get this all crooked again," Smooth told me.

"Dude, no! Please don't make it any more crooked. You've done enough damage and honestly, it is all my fault for being such a wuss. I shouldn't have avoided her in the first place. The longer I waited the harder it became to talk to her and the worse it got. I've got nobody to blame but myself," I told Smooth.

"So you're still my best friend?" Smooth weakly asked.

"Of course, your royal Smoothness. I can't be mad at you for being so smooth. Besides, I should have been a man from the beginning and told her I liked her. The worst that could happen, she could have told me she didn't like me. Or, that she was already promised to the Prince of India, which is where I am at anyways, minus a friend in Logi," I said.

"Sorry again, Franklin. I really didn't mean to nail things up so bad," Smooth apologized.

"That's 'screw' things up, not 'nail' things up, brother Smooth. It's all good. I better get off of here and go hunt up some zzz's. I'll talk to you on the flipside. Night, Smooth. I ain't mad at you," I said tiredly.

"Night, Franklin. Thanks for being an amigo. You're a good dude," Smooth said as he hung up the phone.

15

You Are a Human Corporation

Baron Wufot's
Personal Finance Newsletter for Teens
February 1

You are a human corporation. It is important to view your career or work life as a growing company. Early on in my career, I came to the realization that my career was like a business. I realized that I was a human company or a human corporation.

As I started improving myself by acquiring more and more personal assets, I realized I was improving my career and benefitting monetarily from acquiring more personal assets. Examples of personal assets are degrees, certifications, and proprietary knowledge. The more personal assets I obtained, the more valuable I became to an employer and the more money I could potentially make. As a result, life became easier and I had more leverage at work to decide how I used my time to make the company better.

What is an asset?

An asset is a tangible or intangible resource that produces money. A tangible asset is something you can touch, for example, an office building, land, vehicles, and a machine in a factory. An intangible asset is something untouchable but still creates money, for example, a patent, computer software, trademarks, proprietary knowledge, and trade secrets.

When you begin to think of yourself as a human corporation, you set a goal to acquire as many useful assets as possible. By acquiring personal assets, you increase the value of your human corporation. I track my human corporation assets with two lists.

The first list I keep a running total of all of my current assets that I have acquired over the years. These are assets that I have already obtained.

My second list is a list of human corporation assets I would like to acquire in the future. These are assets I think will make me more valuable to an employer or to the world.

Below are the two lists I have maintained over the years to track my assets as a human corporation.

Baron Wufot, the Human Corporation

Current Assets List

- » Bachelor's Degree in Finance
- » Master's Degree in Business Administration
- » Series 7—General Securities Representative
- » Series 66—Certified Investment Adviser
- » Toastmasters Club—public speaking
- » Graphic Design Experience—responsible for the design of sales collateral
- » Published four books on personal finance
- » Publish monthly personal finance newsletter for teens
- » Blog
- » Speak Spanish fluently
- » Photographer
- » Office building
- » House
- » Car
- » Brokerage investment account
- » 401K savings account
- » Bartending and waiting tables to gain experience in public speaking

Future Assets to Acquire or Continued Education

- » Statistical Analysis
- » Public Speaking
- » Big Data
- » Negotiation Skills
- » Project Management
- » Mental Elasticity
- » Creativity Engineer

In my opinion, the two most important skills to learn and to continually improve are public speaking and personal finance. I am an active member of the local Toastmasters International Club, which continues to help me improve my public speaking. As for continually working to improve my knowledge of finance and personal finance, I spend the majority of my working hours studying this topic and I am the first to admit that it is a bottomless pit of knowledge. You can never stop learning.

Constructing your current and future human corporation asset lists are a great exercise for everyone to do. I have these lists taped above my desk as a regular reminder. Each month, I make it a point to review them and make any necessary updates. Self-improvement is a worthwhile journey in which to invest. I highly suggest taking the time to figure out what you want to do with your life and figure out the direction to head to accomplish your goal.

If any of you kiddos would like to share your Human Corporation Asset Lists with me, I would love to see them. I don't expect you as a teenager to have lengthy lists, so don't worry about it if you can only come up with two or three assets for each list.

Now, for the moment you have all been waiting for!

Update: High School Stock Market Competition—February

	Name	Total	City, State
1.	ImShortButImLong	$11,900.23	New York, NY
2.	Smootherrific	$11,805.72	St. Louis, MO
3.	SmallCapWonder	$11,517.34	New York, NY
4.	TheBull	$11,513.87	Seattle, WA
5.	GoodTilCancelled	$11,502.87	Baton Rouge, LA

Thank you for taking time out of your day to make your life better. You kiddos are what us old people envy. Time is on your side and not mine.

Yours truly,
Baron Wufot

Compounding Interest Fun Fact: Your money will double every ten years! That is assuming a 7% rate of return, which is the historical average return of the S&P 500 index.

"Who is this guy 'ImShortButLong' and how is he in first place? What does that even mean 'ImShortButLong'?" Smooth complained as he walked into the club meeting. He was fired up today after getting the latest Baron Wufot newsletter and finding out he had fallen to second place in the High School Stock Market Competition. "Is this ImShortButLong some kind of leprechaun with a long nose? I don't get it!"

"Take it easy, your royal Smoothness. I think his or her name is referring to a style of investing. This kid must really know what he or she is doing in order to be short-selling stocks."

"The name 'ImShortButLong' sounds like a carnival name to me. I saw this circus one time in Booneville, where this little goblin was shot out of a cannon and somehow turned into a tall skinny version of himself. It was a good trick. Maybe, that is what this name is referring to," Malibu Martin added.

"Stop, stop, stop. You guys are out of your minds. The name 'ImShortButLong' has to do with the type of investments this kid is making. When you are 'long,' it means you can expect the stock price of a stock you own to go up over time."

"Having a 'short' stock is the opposite of having a 'long' stock. When a stock is 'short,' the investor never takes ownership of the stock, but instead borrows the stock with the intention of selling the stock and then repurchasing it at a lower price. The investor makes the difference in the amount the stock drops. Shortselling a stock is an extremely advanced way to invest in stocks. I don't fully understand how it is done, but I will try to draw you a picture to demonstrate it," I told the group and began to draw an example on the dry erase board.

Long Position

» **Buy long** at $10 ↑↑↑↑ **Stock goes up to** $15 per share and you make a $5 profit or 50% return

» **Buy long** at $10 ↓↓↓↓ **Stock drops to** $5 for a $5 loss or 50% loss in your investment

Note: When you are "long" on a stock, you make money when it goes up in value and you lose money when it goes down in value. Again, **taking a "long" position** means you will profit from an increase in the stock price. This is the traditional type of investment that you are familiar with. Calling it "long" is just another name for investing in a stock you intend to keep for the long term.

Short Position

» **Sell short** at $10 a share ↓↓↓↓ **the stock goes down and you buy it back at** $5 a share for a $5 profit or 50% return

» **Sell short** at $10 ↑↑↑↑ **the stock goes up to** $15 a share for a loss of $5 or 50% loss in your investment

Note: When you are "short" on a stock, you make money when the stock goes down in value and you lose money when it goes up in value. It is the opposite of being "long" a stock. Selling a stock "short" is extremely risky because you can lose an infinite amount of money if the stock keeps going up because the stock can go up infinitely. Shorting a stock is a very advanced investment tool and is usually only used by professional money managers.

Short-selling defined

Short-selling is the sale of a security that is not owned by the seller or that the seller has borrowed. Short-selling is motivated by the belief that a stock's price will decline, enabling it to be bought back at a lower price to make a profit. Short-selling may be prompted by speculation or by the desire to hedge the downside risk of a long position in the same security or a related one. Since the risk of loss on a short sale is theoretically infinite, short-selling should only be used by experienced traders who are familiar with the risks.

"So buying a stock (aka, taking a long position) is kind of like in football when you tell your wide receiver to 'go long' for a pass?" Smooth questioned.

"That's a good way to remember it. So if the wide receiver catches the football and scores a touchdown, then the whole team benefits by getting six points and the opportunity to kick an extra point," I explained a little bit further. "Honestly, we shouldn't even be having a conversation about the difference between being 'long' or 'short' with a stock. We should only be thinking about buying a stock for the long term. Leave the 'short'-selling of a stock to the professional money managers. All we will end up doing if we try to 'short' a stock is to screw it up royally. That means you, Smooth!"

"This kid 'ImShortButLong is from New York and I bet he or she has a parent who is a stockbroker or some other kind of a professional investor," Logi informed us. "I bet the kid's parent is even advising the kid on how to win the competition."

"That's a good grab," Malibu agreed. "Although, our boy Franklin Fi knows all about this stuff and he's only sixteen years old. I don't remember Baron Wufot mentioning anything about 'shorting' stocks in his newsletter. How do you know about this stuff, Franklin?"

"Guess. I'll give you a hint. It starts with the letter '**L**' and ends with the letter '**Y**.' Any guesses?" I joked.

"Your **LooneY LandladY LiterallY** told you at the **LaboratorY**," Smooth blurted out. "That's my attempt to kill one bird with four stones!"

"You are a maniac, Smooth. None of those words make sense and they have never been used together in the history of the universe, " I said as I was laughing my face off. "And no, I didn't learn about shorting stocks from my **LooneY LandladY**."

"Then you learned about shorting stocks from the **LovelY LunchladY** in the **LavatorY**," Smooth guessed again.

"You are out of control. No more guesses for you. I learned about shorting stocks from a **LibrarY** book called *Hedge Funds Explained* by Marly Hunger.

Apparently, Marly Hunger is Baron Wufot's business partner. Here, take a look at it." I said as I threw the book on the table. Smooth quickly snatched it up and started flipping through the pages.

"I just thought the library was where you went to pick up smart chicks," Malibu Martin croaked in his frog-like voice.

"I wish that was the case because I have spent way too many hours there and have never picked up a girl at the library," I told Malibu Martin.

"Can I borrow this book on hedge funds?" Smooth asked.

"Sure, I've already read it. Smooth, just bring it back by next Wednesday before it is due. I don't want to have to pay a late fee," I said to Smooth.

"That explains why you know a little bit about shorting stocks," Logi added. She had been quiet up to this point and for a good reason. We still hadn't discussed what was going on between us and there was a lot of tension. "A hedge fund is an investment company that is known for taking both sides of the trade, both the 'short' and 'long' side of the trade. My aunt works for a hedge fund in Chicago and she tried to explain it to me. It's super complicated stuff and I still fully don't understand. Basically, she told me not to worry about shorting stocks and that I should first figure out how to buy good stocks to hold onto for a long period of time."

"Logi, I ended up taking your advice," Smooth cut in. "I decided to try and preserve my lead by taking a position in an index fund. As you can see, all that did was put me back in second place."

"My penny stocks tanked this past month," Malibu Martin stated. "I went from number two in the competition to dropping way back to the middle of the pack. My virtual portfolio lost 30% this past month. Though, it's all good. I switched out a couple of my underperforming penny stocks for some new penny stocks that are doing better."

"Dude, you are quite the hustler. I don't have the stomach to watch my stocks go up and down like that," I said. "Logi and I are in the middle of the pack with our portfolios up about 4% since the competition started, which is actually really good considering the competition has only been running for a little over three months now."

"You are still in striking distance, Smooth. So don't worry about ImShortButLong, he or she will slip up," Logi reassured him.

"The win is so close, I can taste it on the tip of my nose," Smooth said. Sometimes I can't tell if he is serious or really just can't control what comes out of his mouth.

"I think you meant to say that you can taste it on your lips," Malibu corrected him.

"That's what I said, sheesh!" Smooth responded. "I've got a big decision to make this month. There are about two months left in the competition. I can either hold tight with my current portfolio with the hope that ImShortButLong blows it. Or I can roll the dice on a couple of new penny stocks with the hope they will take off and double before the competition is over."

"Whoa, cowboy, stocks don't double in a couple of months," I cautioned Smooth. "Dude, you better take a night or two to think about what you are going to do. You're not in a bad position. Plus, it never turns out good when you buy and sell stocks based on emotions."

"Okay, boss. You're probably right, I should think this one over and try not to pull a SMOOTH move this close to the end of the competition," Smooth responded.

There was no way Smooth was going to wait two days to make a decision. My intuition told me he was going to walk straight out of this meeting and immediately bet on a couple of penny stocks. Malibu Martin just got burnt by penny stocks and Smooth was going to do the same thing if he wasn't careful. But there was nothing I could do to stop him. Besides, he didn't earn the nickname "Smooth" solely for the fact that it was his last name. He was known for not thinking his decisions through and responding like a wild dog in a chicken coup.

"How about we move on?" I suggested. "In his newsletter, Baron Wufot suggested that we put together a couple of lists. What do you all think about doing those two exercises as homework for next month's meeting?"

"What lists are you talking about? All of this homework for the club is cutting into my face time at the mall," Malibu Martin said. Face time is what he calls chasing chicks or being seen by chicks.

"The Baron suggested we put together a 'Human Corporation Assets' list." I continued. "The first list he suggested we put together was a list of our current assets. Then he suggested we put together a second list of assets we would like to obtain in the next five years."

"This Lord Baron Wufot sure knows how to challenge us," Malibu Martin unenthusiastically stated.

"It's kind of fun. I don't think I would have learned any of this if it wasn't for him and Franklin," Smooth added. "Count me in on the homework. It's weird, but I actually like doing homework for the club. I feel like I am learning stuff I will actually use in life. Besides, how can I ignore advice from the richest man in the solar system?"

"Ain't that the truth!" I agreed with Smooth. Doing homework for the club was actually exhilarating. Why can't all learning be that way?

We all agreed to do the homework for next month's meeting. It was obvious that Baron was challenging his readers to improve themselves by learning what nobody taught him when he was a teenager. I welcomed his advice and was always searching for more. I was in the second month of saving money from my job and my brokerage savings account was up to $720. I had been putting half of my savings into an index fund. With the other half, I intended to invest in stocks, but hadn't got up the nerve to buy my first stock.

"Alright chaps, time to finish up before the bell rings," Professor Crutchfield warned us.

"Anybody want to add anything before the bell rings?" I asked as the meeting was adjourning.

Brrring!!! Brrring!!! Brrring!!!
Brrring!!! Brrring!!! Brrring!!!

"Guess not, see you losers later," Malibu joked as he and Smooth rushed out of the room together. Then Profesor Crutchfield snatched up his papers and walked out. Before I knew it, I was alone with Logi in the classroom.

As I was putting my things away in my backpack, Logi put her hand on my hand to stop me.

"Do you have a second to talk?" Logi asked.

I was stunned, my heart was pounding so hard and loud that I could barely hear what she was saying.

"Franklin, you are one of my best friends…"

THUMP THUMP THUMP THUMP THUMP THUMP

"I didn't fully realize what I was doing to you…"

THUMP THUMP THUMP THUMP THUMP THUMP

"I never thought of you as more than just a friend, until…"

THUMP THUMP THUMP THUMP THUMP THUMP

"Until, until this last month when we stopped talking. Then it seemed like we stopped hanging out together…"

I was frozen, part of me wanted to run home and hide in my closet for the rest of my life. The other part of me wanted to tell Logi how I felt about her, that I thought she was the most beautiful person in the world, that she made me nervous every time I saw her. That I liked her like spicy red curry, not spicy green curry and that I have a drunken noodle for her.

THUMP THUMP THUMP THUMP THUMP THUMP

"I missed your smiling face. The more I thought about

you, the more I realized I do have feelings for you, as more than just a friend…"

I was frozen solid, but I knew I had to say something or I was going to regret it for the rest of my life.

"Um, uh, well, uh, uh…spicy green curry…no drunken noodle…Smooth move," I mumbled.

She embraced me in a friendly hug as she began to laugh. And then I started to laugh and relax a little bit. We laughed and laughed until both of us had tears in our eyes. My heart was still thumping so hard I could barely hear myself think. Then I realized I was hugging Logi. We hugged and laughed for what seemed like forever. I think it was our way of acknowledging how much we cared for each other.

"I have feelings for you as well, even if you only see me as spicy green curry," Logi said between laughs.

"I have no idea how Smooth came up with spicy green curry or any of the other food analogies for that matter. He's a mess sometimes, but I love him," I told her.

"I don't really know how to go about this whole friendship to relationship thing, so can we just take it slow?" Logi asked.

"Of course, I promise to keep my drunken noodle to myself," I said in laughter.

We laughed some more until we realized we were late for our next class. As we ran out of the room together, it occurred to me I was holding her hand. It seemed so natural.

THUMP THUMP THUMP THUMP THUMP THUMP

16

A Hug For Your Lips

I was flying high and everything was looking up. That afternoon, I was working at the Paddle Department Store. It was a slow afternoon and I found myself having a hard time keeping my mind on the job and not on Logi. I couldn't believe finally I actually had a girlfriend. But what does that mean, "a girlfriend"? Now that Logi and I had confessed our love (or like) for each other, it wasn't obvious to me what was next. Should I tell Malibu and Smooth? Do I ask Logi out on a date? Am I supposed to buy her flowers?

"Hey honey, can you grab me two of those large pink towels from the top shelf?" a sweet old lady asked while politely disrupting my daydream.

"Um, yeah of course," I responded dumbly.

"Is everything okay honey? You seem a little out of it. Should I ask someone else to help me?" the sweet old lady prodded.

"Yeah, everything is okay. Well actually, that's not entirely true. You see, I just got my first girlfriend and well, I have no idea what to do next," I answered. "But that's probably too much information. You said you wanted the pink towels or the blue ones?"

"Oh, to be young and in love again," she said. "I have been married for nearly fifty years. The best advice I can give you is to just be there as a friend for her. If she needs help with something, make sure to go above and beyond to help her out. And, once in a while, surprise her with flowers. Oh, if you buy her flowers, make sure to write a nice long note. All women love handwritten notes. The flowers might die after a week, but your letter will last forever. It's something that will always be kept around and it captures a feeling in time."

"Be a friend, go above and beyond to help her out, buy her flowers, and write her a love letter from time to time. I think I can do that!" I said with a grin.

"And don't forget that Valentine's Day is right around the corner," she reminded me. "Now, can you get those pink towels from the top shelf?"

"There's no chance of me ever forgetting Valentine's Day, both my girlfriend and I share the same birthday, which happens to fall exactly on Valentine's Day," I told the her. "And here you go, two blue towels. Sorry about the delay."

Valentine's Day

Logi and I decided to meet at the St. Louis Botanical Garden for Valentine's Day (and both of our birthdays). Every year, they have an orchid show on Valentine's Day and this year we had an excuse to check it out together. Logi had been teasing me all week about a birthday surprise she had for me. Of course, you can guess where my male, nearly seventeen-year-old mind was running to. I was hoping for a birthday kiss and I had even been practicing in the mirror at home when nobody was looking. Talk about an awkward exercise.

"Hey Logi," I said as I gave her a hug at the entrance of the botanical garden. I thought to myself, does a hug count as making it to first base, or is that only a kiss? I was so bad at this boyfriend business.

"Hey Franklin Fi, great idea. I love orchids, they're my favorite flower. I can't wait to see the orchid show," Logi told me.

As a gag gift for Valentine's Day, I thought it would be funny to buy her some orchids for the orchid show. I had even written her a long love letter, just like the sweet old lady suggested.

"Here, Happy Valentine's Day! I brought these for you," I said as I handed her the orchids. It was all I could do to not laugh. At this point, I don't think she fully got the joke. I bought her orchids to bring to the world's largest orchid show.

"Franklin, I love them," Logi exclaimed. "I have never been given flowers before by anybody but my dad. I'll never forget this. Plus, orchids are my favorite."

She still hadn't caught on to my humor yet. I was starting to think it was going to be one of those jokes that was only funny to me.

"I also wrote you a letter, but it's no big deal. Happy Birthday and Happy Valentine's Day!!! I love that our birthdays are both on Valentine's Day. I wonder if there are any other couples out there who share a birthday on Valentine's Day?" I questioned.

As Logi read the letter, her eyes started to tear up and I

thought she was going to cry right there on the steps of the botanical garden. I wrote the letter from my heart. This was the first time I realized how strong Logi's feelings were for me. We had only been dating for a few weeks, but we had been friends for years. I guess, like me, our feelings were always there for each other.

When we walked into the orchid show, Logi finally got the joke. She was holding a bouquet of orchids in the middle of a zillion orchids on display. She immediately started cracking up!

"Kind of like bringing sand to the beach, very funny. Franklin, now I can relate to how Smooth feels when he pulls a smooth move. Did you do this on purpose?" she asked.

"Of course not," I joked.

Logi handed me the orchids and I ended up carrying them around the orchid exhibit. I definitely got some funny looks as we walked around the botanical gardens, but I didn't really care. It looked like we had been picking orchids throughout the show to make our own bouquet. Occasionally, I would bend down and act as if I had just picked an orchid right from the ground and then I would hand Logi an orchid from her bouquet. She would turn bright red no matter how many times I did it throughout the show. It was hilarious.

Afterward, Logi and I walked outside and she hailed a taxi cab. Before she would let me get into the cab, she stuck her head into the cab and told the driver where she wanted to go. At that point, my heart started beating even faster. Where were we going?

The taxi ended up dropping us off at the St. Louis City Garden next to the St. Louis Arch. The garden looks like something you would find in London or Paris. It definitely doesn't look like something you would find in St. Louis,

Misery. At the end of the garden is the centerpiece of St. Louis, the Gateway Arch.

Since it was the middle of February, the gardens had been simplified for the winter snow and there wasn't anything in bloom. Nonetheless, it was a beautiful setting for what would turn into one of the best nights of my life.

We walked until we arrived at the Gateway Arch and then had a seat on the stairs beneath it overlooking the Mississippi River.

If you are not familiar with the Gateway Arch, it is definitely worth traveling to St. Louis to see. The arch is built out of stainless steel and towers 630 feet above the city of St. Louis. It is the tallest arch constructed by man in the solar system. The arch is known as the gateway to the west.

"Happy birthday, Franklin," Logi said as she handed me a gift. At this point, we were bundled up in our winter coats and sitting close to each other.

I began to open it and quickly realized it was a book. As I ripped away the wrapping paper, I saw it was a first edition copy of Baron Wufot's first book. It was probably worth at least a few hundred dollars. I read it at the library, but I didn't have the funds to actually own a copy of the first edition. As I opened the book, I saw there was a message on the inside of the cover. The message read:

Dear Franklin,

If I could give you one piece of advice, it would be to never stop creating and learning. The day you lose your imagination is the day you die. Happy Birthday, kiddo!

Your friend,
Baron Wufot

"How in the world did you get Baron Wufot to sign this for me? Logi, this is the best gift ever. You didn't have to do this for me. The book alone must have cost you a small fortune and then getting him to sign it. Come on, you're too much. Look, he even calls me his friend. I am a friend to the Baron. This is the most amazing thing ever. How did you pull this off?"

"Oh, I know people," Logi told me with a huge grin on her face.

"Thank you! You are the only person in the universe who would know to get this for me. You're the best!" I said.

Then, I leaned in to give her a big hug as thanks, but she didn't go for the hug. She opened her mouth for a kiss and I was totally caught off guard. She had her mouth open and my mouth was closed. It was a disaster. Everything was moving in slow motion. I awkwardly corrected and started to kiss Logi, tongue and all. This was the moment I had prepared my whole life for. I had spent hours upon hours watching film for research. My first kiss. I thought I was the closest thing to an expert one could be on the subject of kissing, without actually kissing anybody. Unfortunately, I was wrong. The lack of experience was too much to overcome. I botched my first kiss badly, but I was on first base! I got my first kiss, from Logi Laru, on my seventeenth birthday, under the St. Louis Arch. It was a day I will never forget.

17

Time is Your Most Valuable Asset

Baron Wufot's
Personal Finance Newsletter for Teens
March 1

Earnings Season

'Tis the season for earnings! Four times a year, large publicly traded companies release their quarterly earnings report. The earnings season starts after each financial quarter ends, therefore January, April, July, and October are the months when most companies report their financial numbers. On a company's quarterly earnings report, you can find information like a company's revenue or earnings, expenses for the quarter, Net Profit Margin, amount of cash the company has at its disposal, and many other financial numbers. These numbers are of great use in determining the financial health of a company. Earnings season acts as a barometer for investors. It allows investors to gauge whether or not they want to invest in the company.

Financial Analysts are people who work on Wall Street and use the reported information to figure out how much a company is really worth or how much the stock will be worth in the future. Financial Analysts will publish their estimates and advise investors which company's stock they should buy, hold, or sell.

A single earnings report can drive the company's near-term stock price. Earnings trends or a series of quarterly earnings over a longer period of time drives the company's long-term stock price. If a company is consistently increasing its earnings month over month, the stock will eventually follow. You want to buy companies that have positive earnings growth and consistently outperform the financial analyst's estimates.

I like to keep a watch list of the stocks I would like to buy sometime in the future. On that watch list, I track key statistics such as the Price to Earnings Ratio and the Net Profit Margin. I also keep track of when the company is scheduled to report their earnings next. As an investor, you don't get many opportunities to gauge how smoothly a company is performing. A quarterly earnings report is your best opportunity to gain insight into a company.

Now, for the moment you have all been waiting for!

Update: High School Stock Market Competition—March

	Name	Total	City
1.	ImShortButImLong	$12,254.98	New York, NY
2.	Smootherrific	$11,975.34	St. Louis, MO
3.	TheBull	$11,613.23	Seattle, WA
4.	DivOrDie	$11,524.27	Charlotte, NC
5.	InItToWinIt	$11,482.87	Miami, FL

With less than two months to go, the competition is very close. Much like a professional basketball game, this competition is going to come down to who plays or invests the best in the last quarter. Be cautious, because earnings season is right around the corner. Earnings season is a very risky part of the year to make short-term trades. It is impossible to know if the company is going to report positive or negative earnings, so I am suggesting you try to avoid any companies that are reporting earnings on or around the end of the competition.

Thank you all for taking time out of your day to make your life better. You kiddos are what us old people envy. Time is on your side and not mine.

Yours truly,
Baron Wufot

Compounding Interest Fun Fact: If you were to save $10 per month, earn 7% interest compounded each month, and do that continually for 48 years until retirement, you would have contributed a total of $5,770 into savings, but the account would be worth $47,444 due to compounding interest. By taking advantage of compounding interest over a long period of time, your account adds up faster than you think!

"Brah, how is it your new penny stocks didn't put you in the lead or totally capsize your portfolio?" Malibu Martin questioned Smooth. They were the first to arrive at the club meeting and had been waiting for Logi and Franklin Fi for a few minutes. "I thought for sure your portfolio would make a big move in one direction or the other."

"Well bro-hamwich sandwich, your Smoothness took Logi's and Franklin's advice and invested part of my virtual portfolio into an index fund. I decided it would be stupid to gamble with my portfolio by investing in penny stocks," Smooth proudly announced.

"Wait, the smoothest of the Smooths actually stopped to think before making a decision? So, you actually took their advice and played it safe? What fun is that?" Malibu Martin was puzzled.

"Yeah, for once in my life I stopped to think and made the correct decision. It's mind-bending, I know. My prefrontal cortex is on fire. This is the new and improved funky, smoothtastic flavor of your Smoothness," Smooth joked. "Besides, whose advice did you think I was going to take? The advice from Franklin, who spends every free second studying the stock market in the library or the guy who has been blindly gambling on penny stocks?"

"Well, well, well, look who decided to come to the club meeting. If it isn't Mr. and Mrs. Franklin Fi. You two lovebirds are glowing today. Is there something you want to tell us, maybe why you are late for the meeting?" Malibu Martin said.

"Oh stop it, sorry we're late. What were you guys discussing?" Logi asked.

"If you really want to know, Smooth and I were wagering whether you two lovebirds were making out in the parking lot or in the janitor's closet. So which is it?" Malibu Martin jokingly croaked in his froggy voice.

"Very funny, I see that Franklin and I are going to be the butt of all of your jokes from here on out. Well, sorry to disappoint you, we don't make out in parking lots and storage closets. I've tried, but apparently, Franklin is too classy for that." joked Logi. "If you can't beat them, join them."

"Actually, Brandi from the school newspaper stopped us in the hallway and asked if she could write an article on the Stock Market Club for next month's newspaper," I told them.

"That's great news, maybe the exposure will help us next year to grow our club roster 50% to six total members!" joked Smooth.

"Actually, we told her Smooth was the true story. Smooth, she didn't even know about the National Stock Market Competition, let alone that you were in second place with less than two months to go."

"Does that mean I'm going to be famous?" Smooth asked excitedly.

"If you win, yes, you are probably going to be the talk

of the school. That street goes both ways though, don't pull a smooth move or you will go down in school history as the infamous Sam Smooth," I warned him.

"Ahh, you guys. You didn't have to go and make me a star. Now I'm going to have to start searching for a public relations firm to handle all of my day-to-day contact with all of the media outlets. Who knows, maybe next they'll want to turn my story into a bibliography that will eventually be followed up by a movie deal. I can see it now. It will be titled 'Smoothness' and I will be played by Justin Sleeper, the famous rockstar." Smooth said with a twinkle in his eyes.

"Slow down, cowboy. I think you meant to say one day someone will write a biography about you, not a bibliography," I corrected him. "By the way, Smooth. I saw you managed to remain in the top five of the competition. I take it you stayed away from the penny stocks. I thought for sure you were going to pull a smooth move and get caught up in the hustle of penny stocks."

"And defy your advice, Franklin?" Smooth responded. "You're just about the only person I know who understands the first thing about the stock market. No offense, Malibu. The more I thought about it, the more I realized the smart thing to do was to take Franklin's advice. I dropped back a position to second place, but I'm still in the competition. If I win the $10,000, it could change my whole life."

"Logi and I will do what we can to help you out. I'm glad you took the time to think your decision through. We're all capable of improving ourselves," I told Smooth.

"Now we've got earnings season to worry about. Clearly, I think Baron Wufot was giving us all a warning to expect some volatility in the market during earnings season," Logi added.

"Good point, we should all probably take a look at our holdings and write down their earnings date. That way we are prepared for the quarterly reports. As the Baron said, the companies tend to make a move one way or another on the day they report their earnings. Speaking of reporting, should we all go over our 'Human Corporation Asset List' homework?" I suggested.

"Sure thing, boss. I found it was a challenge trying to come up with my current assets list. After I gave it some thought, I got the hang of it. This exercise definitely altered the perception of my life," Malibu Martin confessed.

"I'm excited to see what you came up with. How about I get the ball rolling and go first?" I told the group.

"Whew, I'm glad you said that," Smooth said.

"Alright, here is my list," I said as I passed out a sheet of paper with my "Human Corporation" assets listed on it.

1. Time is my most valuable asset. I feel very lucky to have discovered the teachings of Baron Wufot. By starting to invest at the age of sixteen, it allows me to take advantage of compounding interest for a longer period of time than if I had started later in life. Time is an intangible asset.

2. My brokerage savings account is my second "Human Corporation" asset. I have been able to grow my brokerage savings account to over $1,500 by saving over 60% of each of my paychecks. It's amazing how fast it adds up! I never thought I would have more than $1,000 to my name. Now I am on my way to $2,000. Here's what my most up-to-date Profit and Loss Statement looks like:

Dec. 1—Financial Results for Franklin Fi
> **Profit:** $393.19 − $167.12 = $226.07
> **Savings Rate:** $226.07 ÷ $393.19 = 57.50%
> **Total Net Worth:** $226.07
> **Amount in Index Fund:** $113.69
> **Amount in Stocks:** $113.51

Jan. 1—Financial Results for Franklin Fi
> **Profit:** $768.45 − $277.89 = $490.56
> **Savings Rate:** $490.56 ÷ $768.45 = 63.84%
> **Total Net Worth:** $717.76
> **Amount in Index Fund:** $360.97
> **Amount in Stocks:** $360.38

Feb. 1—Financial Results for Franklin Fi
> **Profit:** $689.09 − $232.47 = $456.62
> **Savings Rate:** $456.62 ÷ $689.09 = 66.26%
> **Total Net Worth:** $1,177.97
> **Amount in Index Fund:** $592.42
> **Amount in Stocks:** $591.44

Mar. 1—Financial Results for Franklin Fi
> **Profit:** $617.23 − $225.87 = $391.36
> **Savings Rate:** $391.36 ÷ $617.23 = 63.41%
> **Total Net Worth:** $1,575.22
> **Amount in Index Fund:** $792.21
> **Amount in Stocks:** $790.90

3. My bicycle (aka Disco) is my third and final "Human Corporation" asset. It's not that it is worth much from a monetary standpoint, but it is invaluable to me. It allows me to get to where I need to be. The best part

is that it basically costs me nothing for transportation. With a car payment, insurance payment, and gas fill-up every few days, it would cost me around $300 per month. If that was the case, I would have next to nothing in my brokerage savings account. All of my money would be going to the bank to pay off a car loan. An ancillary benefit of riding my bicycle everywhere is that I get the exercise and happiness that comes along with it.

"That pretty much sums up my 'Human Corporation' current assets report. It was a lot harder than I thought to come up with three assets I could trade for money. I think at our age, it is probably going to be easier to list intangible assets. In other words, untouchable, intellectual assets," I told the group.

"Well, that is a tough act to follow, but I'll give it my best pitch," Smooth stated.

"Smootherific, I think you meant to say you will give it your best shot, as in a basketball shot," Malibu Martin corrected him.

"Sheesh, that is what I said, my best kick," Smooth said.

"Okay, you clowns, let's focus on the task at hand," I suggested.

"Here are my top three 'Human Corporation' current assets," Smooth told us as he handed us his homework.

1. Comic Book Collection: I have over two thousand comic books and I estimate my collection is probably worth over $5,000. Five thousand big ones. Five thousand kangaroos.

2. Car skilz: My dad and I have bought three hotrods, fixed them up, and sold them for a profit. So number dos, I am a novice car mechanic. I'm sure if I needed to, I could go get a job repairing cars or working at a grease shop.

3. House building skilz: My dad and I built the house our family lives in. It took us three years and we practically built it from the foundation up. We dug the basement and laid the foundation. I helped with the electrical, operated some big machines, and even learned to lay down a pipe system.

"Boom! As you can see, I am a walking, talking asset," Smooth concluded.

"Wait, that means you are a Smooth operator when it comes to laying pipe. You are a man of many talents, your royal smoothness," Malibu joked.

"Yeah, I guess you could put it like that. Laying pipe is my name and operating heavy equipment is my game. Hey hey hey, funktastic, smoothtastic ain't afraid of no fame," Smooth rapped as he bounced and tucked like a hip-hop hood would do in a music video.

"You guys are a riot," Logi said while cracking up. "That's great work, Smooth. You might want to think about adding your dance moves as number four on your current assets list. No doubt in my mind you could make some money shaking that rump shaker for some buckaroos, or as you would say, kangaroos!"

"You all continue to amaze me. Every time our club meets, I am blown away by what we come up with and learn from each other. Good work, brother Smooth, you are one bad dude," I added.

"Alright, Logi Laru, do you want to go next or do you want me to?" Malibu asked.

"Let's save the best for last, I'll go next and then you can be the grand finale," Logi responded. "Here it goes!"

1. Yoga and Meditation: I have been studying yoga and meditation all of my life and one day I would like to teach what I have learned to others.

2. Public Speaking: This is an asset I value very much and have a lot of pride in. I have been going to Toastmasters International for the last three years. If you are not familiar with Toastmasters, it is a public speaking club that teaches you how to prepare and give a presentation to a group. I think public speaking might be the most important skill to possess in the workforce. If you know how to command a room or a conference hall filled with people, then you have a skill almost any company desires. Unfortunately, it is a skill that most of us are never taught, which can do more harm than good.

3. Personal Finance: This is a skill every individual will need to use in their lifetime. For the life of me, I can not figure out why this skill is not a required class in every high school across the nation. So I have made it my own personal goal to learn about saving, car loans, credit cards, student loans, and retirement accounts.

"That's all I got. I like this activity, because it is proactive and helped me think about what is important in life," Logi said.

"Franklin Fi, why do I have the feeling you find Logi's

last current asset to be sexy. I can see it all over your face," Malibu Martin said. And he was right, he had caught me red-handed.

"Stop, I was just thinking about how much better her assets were than mine," I said, but I knew as soon as the words came out of my mouth I was going to catch heat for it.

"Logi does have nice assets, you said it first. And I take it you lost that drunken noodle of yours over a little sexy, finance talk. Franklin, you are the only person I know in the universe who gets turned on by a girl muttering the words 'personal finance.' You are a freak of nature, brother!" Malibu Martin joked.

Malibu Martin was right, I don't think there is anything sexier in this world than when Logi talks personal finance. But honestly, she could talk about any subject and I would get excited.

"WEIGHING IN AT A ROBUST 125 POUNDS, HAILING FROM ST. LOUIS, MISERY, WITH A RECORD OF ZERO WINS AND ZERO LOSSES, FIGHTING IN THE BLUE TRUNKS, THE MALIBU OF MISSOURI! THE KID THAT HAS MORE DATES THAN A CALENDAR. THE ONE. THE ONLY. MALIBU MARTIN! NOW LET'S GET READY TO MUMBLE" Smooth announced as if he was introducing a boxer at Madison Square Garden.

"I am the greatest, the quickest, fast as fast can be. You'll never catch me. Are you all ready to have your mind blown?" Malibu Martin said as he shadowboxed in the classroom.

"If your 'Human Corporation' current assets list is half as good as Smooth's introduction, then we are in for a tasty treat. Let's have it, dude," I told Malibu Martin.

"Alright, here it goes. I guess it was only a matter of time before all of you found out. I have a teen fashion vlog with two thousand followers!" Malibu Martin blurted out.

"Wait, what did you just say?" I asked.

"I have a teen fashion video blog, aka vlog, with two thousand followers. Do you understand the words coming out of my mouth?" Malibu clarified. "Last summer when I was in Malibu, my cousin and I came up with this crazy idea to start a teen fashion vlog. We were out shopping one day and probably had one too many cold brew coffees when we came up with this crazy idea to start a vlog with us as the hosts. At first, it was kind of a joke. We posted two or three videos and nothing happened. Then one morning we woke up and we had five hundred new followers. It became obvious there really wasn't anything like our vlog on the web, so we started to take it more seriously. By the end of the summer, we were posting and reviewing new designers on a weekly basis. At first, I was too embarrassed to tell all of you because I was afraid of what you would say. Then after a while, it became easier to keep it from you than to share it with you. But once we started talking about 'Human Corporation' assets, I knew this was the perfect opportunity to tell you all about my vlog."

"Dude, that is awesome. I didn't think you were capable of keeping a secret of that caliber. I'm impressed!" I told Malibu Martin. It's hard putting yourself out there. I can only imagine how hard it was for Malibu Martin to tell us about his vlog, knowing we would want to see him in action.

"Alright, here are my three 'Human Corporation' current assets," Malibu said as he passed out a piece of paper.

1. Style: I have been researching fashion my whole life and I consider myself somewhat of a fashion expert at this point. Through the introduction of my vlog, I have started to realize my fashion sense can be monetized and therefore it is an asset.

2. Website Design and Vlogging: By starting my own vlog, I learned how to build and manage a website and a vlog channel. It has turned into a lot of work and as a result, I have been exposed to what it takes to run a business. Creating fresh content is a process that takes weeks of planning before I can actually take it live on my vlog.

3. Social Media: I have had to become a social media expert in order to market my vlog. All of my hard work to increase my followers has finally started to pay off. Social media is not going anywhere. The knowledge I have gained through building my own brand on social media is invaluable.

"There you have it! Smooth is not going to be the only famous person at St. Louis High," Malibu said in his froggy voice.

"Wow man, I thought I was going to be a star but I think you one-upped me today," Smooth told Malibu. "How in the universe did you keep this a secret for the last six months? I can barely keep a secret for a couple of hours."

"Honestly, it is pretty nerve-racking watching yourself online. I was afraid of what you guys would think of me. Plus, I didn't want the girls at school to think I was a failure because of how my vlog looked. The more followers I got, the more my confidence grew. The 'Human Corporation' asset list was the catalyst, man. It gave me the opportunity to tell you all about my vlog," Malibu Martin confessed to us.

"No one is going to make fun of you," Logi said. "If they do, they've got to mess with me. I am super proud of you. Malibu, you should be very proud of yourself for sticking with this project and seeing it through. There have been a lot of times in my life I would start a project like this, only to see it sputter out after a month or so. One time, I started a blog and only posted twice. It's scary to put yourself out there. Worst of all, you are being judged by people who don't know you and don't have the nerve to risk putting themselves out there by starting their own blog."

"So true, thank you for reinforcing what I have been telling myself all the time. It really helps to hear from someone like you," Malibu Martin responded. "My next step is to continue to review and find upcoming designers to work with. Eventually, I would like to develop an online storefront on my website that would serve as an outlet for up-and-coming designers. My website could be an educational tool, in addition to being a storefront for upcoming fashion trends. I plan to start simple with products like man bags, rucksacks, belts, jewelry, wallets, and hats for teens that you can't find anywhere else. In the beginning, I want to avoid anything that comes in sizes like shirts and pants so I don't have to mess with returned merchandise because the consumer bought the wrong size."

"What's your website or channel?" I asked.

"I'll give you all one guess!" Malibu Martin joked.

"Dude, come on. You know I'm not good at stuff like

this," Smooth responded. "Okay, my guess is that you named your website teenmanstuff."

"That is actually a pretty brilliant name, Smooth. I may have to use that in the future on my website. But no, that is not the name of my website," Malibu told us.

"Come on, we all know you named it MalibuMartin," I guessed.

"Ding ding ding! Spot on, dude. I have all of you to thank for giving me that nickname. I think it is the perfect name for a teen fashion website for dudes," Malibu Martin said proudly.

We looked at his website MalibuMartin and watched his vlog interviews with up-and-coming teen designers. It was actually really cool to see Malibu Martin on screen, he was a natural. Of course, there were parts that were rougher than others, but overall it wasn't bad for a teenager with no budget.

"Malibu, you are a natural. Who does your editing, your makeup, your camera work? It's all done really well," Logi complimented.

"I do most of it, when my cousin isn't around to help me out. Everybody thinks it is easy to start a blog or write a book or start a business. But actually come doing it, it's a lot harder than you can ever imagine." Malibu Martin began to explain. "You see, the problem is that everything we read or see in the major media is done by professional teams, not just one person. So when someone like me does his own vlog, it is very easy to become frustrated. I told myself from day one, I can't expect my vlog to be perfect from the start. I would love to know how many people start a similar project but never actually launch a finished product. It is all super intimidating, and I am still trying to wrap my head around going public and letting the world judge me."

"That's a very mature attitude to understand early on. Most people just start a project on excitement and then once they realize how much work it takes, they quickly retreat. A lot of people would like to be rich and famous. But few of them are willing to take the risk, learn a new skill, and work hard to set themselves apart from the rest." I told the group.

"I learned that making mistakes was a learning opportunity and not a reason to give up or judge myself too harshly." Malibu explained. "When I made a mistake, I consciously decided to write it down in my journal. Once I analyzed the mistake, I write down two to three ways I could improve. It seems simple, but this process has worked for me."

"Malibu, I hope you are blogging about your successful process in creating your website and vlog. Everything you have just told us has been very insightful," Logi continued to reassure him.

"Well, at first I was afraid of the criticism. My posts were sporadic and I didn't post content very often. Then I decided that criticism was another learning opportunity. I started to listen, but I don't take it personally." Malibu continued. "If the criticism is valid, I analyze it, with the intention of improving my website. After all, I want the vlog to be successful. Positive input helps keep the creative juices flowing."

I was super proud of Malibu Martin for having the courage to share his website with us. I could tell he put a lot of thought into when and how to reveal it to us. Revealing his website wasn't an easy thing for him to do.

"Why is it everytime our club meets my mind gets blown? I didn't see this coming. I had no idea." I told them. "We've got a really good thing going. It's an awesome feeling to have a group of friends who enjoy sitting around and discussing ways to improve their lives through hard work. I'm sure you spend a lot of time pondering these thoughts, just like me. The Club gives us a platform to discuss our ideas. We are rapidly improving without even knowing it."

"I feel the same way. You are all awesome," Smooth added. "Before this club, I didn't really ever look forward to coming to school. Now, I actually get excited to come to school at least once a month. I spend a large part of every day thinking and learning about the stock market. It helps me discover how I can improve my life in the future."

"Smooth daddy-kane, you are so awesome for thinking all of this through in order to make the right choices," Logi complimented Smooth.

"Thanks for encouraging me, Logi. I have a hard time keeping all of the facts crooked," Smooth incorrectly stated.

"Your Smoothness, we're just trying to figure this all out, just like you are. You shouldn't feel like an outsider, ponyboy," Malibu Martin told him.

"We've got a little more than ten minutes left before the bell rings. How about we go around the room and name one 'Human Corporation' asset we aspire to improve or perfect in the next year?" I suggested.

"I'll go first," Logi piped up. "I would like to become an expert on spreadsheets in order to update my own financial statements. All of this talk about 'Human Corporation' assets has given me some financial ideas, and spreadsheets is the perfect format for capturing them. Plus, spreadsheets appear to be an important piece of software used extensively in the financial industry. The sooner I can master it, the faster I'll excel in the business world. No pun intended," Logi said.

"Great answer!" I told her. "It's definitely something I need to master as well. Let me know if you find any good books or training videos that would be useful in learning about spreadsheets."

"I'll go next," Malibu announced. "I would like to become a better writer. I can tell my writing has improved over the last six months, but I need to spend some time researching best practices to make my vlog the best it can be! I think I am going to take the Franklin Fi approach by going to the library and checking out every book on becoming a better writer."

"That's a solid answer, Malibu," Smooth complimented. "I'll go next. I would like to become a better public speaker. Logi, would you care if I joined your Toastmasters International group?"

"Of course not!" Logi answered excitedly. "The group could definitely use a little more youth in it. Right now, it is me and a bunch of fifty-year-old professionals, which is perfect for me because they are super supportive and great listeners. I'm sure the rest of the club members would be excited if you joined us."

"Alright, Mr. Fantastic Franklin Fi, you're up, Malibu said.

"Well, I want to learn how to become a bicycle mechanic," I confessed. "I've been thinking of building my own bamboo bike, but haven't really figured out where to start. Like anything, sometimes getting started is the hardest part."

"You should see if that bike shop down the street needs any help," Logi suggested. "What small business wouldn't want some inexpensive help from the brilliant Franklin Fi."

"You all need to stop with the complimentary adjectives, or my head is going to start growing. But, that is a good idea," I told her.

Brrrrriiiiinnnngggggg!!! Brrrrriiiiinnnngggggg!!!
Brrrrriiiiinnnngggggg!!!

"Perfect timing. What a great meeting," I said, putting my stuff into my backpack.

"Yeah, this meeting is always the highlight of my month. Alright, I'm outta here. After a while, crocodiles," Malibu Martin said as he rushed out of the classroom to his next class. On his way out, he gave Professor Crutchfield a high five, which put a big smile on the Prof's face.

"So long, King Kongs," Smooth joked as he ran out. On his way out, he gave Professor Crutchfield's head a light noogie in a playful manner.

"You chaps are something else. Get out of here, Smooth, before I rough you up. Ha-ha-ha-ha!!!" Professor Crutchfield laughed as he scooped up the papers and strolled down the hallway.

"Give a hug, ladybug," I said to Logi, since we were the last two left in the room. And it worked.

I got a quick hug from Logi and while we were embracing she said into my ear, "Thank you for opening up to me, it's not an easy thing to do."

"Isn't that part of it?" I whispered back. I could barely breathe and my heart was pounding.

"Hey, I just remembered. Do you want to join me for disco yoga tomorrow night?" she asked.

"Of course, I would love to," I told her.

"Great, I'll see you there. It starts at eight o'clock," she said as we untangled ourselves and made our way to our next class.

◆———◆✕◆———◆

I met Logi at the yoga studio and of course, she was dressed head-to-toe in a glow-in-the-dark yoga outfit. Logi's mesmerizing, emerald green eyes were set off by her neon pink outfit. And yes, she was the hottest girl in the yoga studio. The few guys there were checking her out and I was still trying to get used to my girlfriend always being stared at. I kept telling myself I couldn't fault them for checking her out, I did the same thing for years. All I could really do is grab her hand every once in a while to indicate that she was with me. I always feel like an animal when I do this, but it is an effective way to show other guys she has a boyfriend…me!

My outfit was definitely an upgrade from my last appearance at disco yoga. I sported black shorts and a black t-shirt with a glow-in-the-dark, sparkly silhouette of Michael Jackson doing the moonwalk. My outfit was set off by glow-in-the-dark sweatbands on my arms, legs, and around my forehead. In any other setting, I would have looked completely ridiculous but at disco yoga, I fit right in. Regardless, everyone looks exactly the same when the lights go out and the strobe lights begin flashing.

My yoga practice had definitely improved over the last few months. At first, I felt very uncoordinated and self-conscious, like everybody was watching me. As I practiced more with Logi and attended more classes, I realized that everybody in class was focused only on themselves. There was absolutely no reason to be embarrassed about my yoga practice, because the point is to focus inwardly and not judge others.

After yoga class, we went to our favorite cafe for tea. Logi had rooibos tea and I had a white tea with mint leaves and honey. White tea has a small amount of caffeine in it, so I was pretty wired. I hadn't eaten much and ninety minutes of a yoga class can be very dehydrating.

Per usual, Logi and I talked and laughed until both of us had to go home. I offered to get us a taxi, but she said her dad was already out and about and expected to pick her up.

That's when I made the mistake of asking what her parents thought of me. To my surprise, Logi said she hadn't really talked to her parents about me. It was kind of a shock to me to think I didn't even exist to her parents.

I bit my tongue and left the topic quickly. But deep down inside, I knew Logi could not say anything to her parents about having an American boyfriend. That is, if she even thought of me as her boyfriend. I didn't really know what she thought of me.

I once read in a book about Hinduism that some Hindu parents do not allow their daughters to marry based on love. Also, some Hindus believe that marriage is not only between individuals but is also a marriage of families.

I thought to myself, it's possible that Logi's family may never accept me because of the differences of our family's beliefs. It was hard to think I could be madly in love with Logi and her parents might never approve of a marriage with someone like me.

As you can imagine, I was heartbroken again. This love thing was more difficult than advertised. Why do I keep doing this to myself knowing what the conclusion would most likely be if I continue down this path?

That night, I made the conscious decision to go along with Logi's secret about me until there was a breaking point or until she decided to tell her parents about me.

18

The Stock Market Doubles Every Ten Years

Baron Wufot's
Personal Finance Newsletter for Teens
April 1

The Rule of 72

The Rule of 72 is a tool used to determine how long an investment will roughly take to double. The Rule of 72 simply states that if you divide 72 by a fixed rate of return, you will roughly get the number of years it will take your original investment to double.

    72 ÷ rate of return = years to double

The stock market has historically returned 7% on average since the year 1950. So how long does it take for an investment in a total market index fund to double? Let's figure that out using the Rule of 72 and an average rate of return of 7%.

$$72 \div 7\% = 10.3 \text{ years}$$

Therefore, the stock market doubles roughly every 10 years. Remember, this is an average and as a result, the market will sometimes double faster than 10 years and sometimes it will double slower than 10 years. But on average, it takes about 10 years for the stock market to double at a 7% average rate of return.

Now let's look at that from a compounding interest point of view.

Initial investment = $10,000
Average rate of return = 7%

Note: notice that the principal balance comes very close to doubling every 10 years.

Year	Balance
0	$10,000.00
1	$10,700.00
2	$11,449.00
3	$12,250.43
4	$13,107.96
5	$14,025.52
6	$15,007.30

7	$16,057.81
8	$17,181.86
9	$18,384.59
10	$19,671.51
11	$21,048.52
12	$22,521.92
13	$24,098.45
14	$25,785.34
15	$27,590.32
16	$29,521.64
17	$31,588.15
18	$33,799.32
19	$36,165.28
20	$38,696.84
30	$76,122.55
40	$149,744.58
50	$294,570.25

Look how powerful compounding interest becomes in the later years, assuming a 7% average rate of return.

Year	Balance	% increase
0	$10,000.00	
1	$10,700.00	7.00%
10	$19,671.51	97%
20	$38,696.84	287%
30	$76,122.55	661%
40	$149,744.58	1397%
50	$294,570.25	2846%

In the years from 0 to 10, you make about $9,671 in the first ten-year period. Now, look at year 30 to year 40, you make $73,622 in a period of ten years. Then, amazingly from year 40 to year 50, you make $144,826 in the last ten-year period. Compounding interest is simply amazing. Kiddos, the takeaway lesson is that the sooner you begin to invest, the better off you'll be in the future. Also, it is not a bad idea to buy index funds with the intention of owning them for as long as possible.

Here are some more examples of the Rule of 72 with higher rates of return.

8%

72 ÷ 8 = 9 years double
at an 8% avg rate of return

10%

72 ÷ 10 = 7.2 years to double
at a 10% avg rate of return

We are nearing the end of the first annual High School Stock Market Competition. I wrote this newsletter to illustrate how you, as a teenager, can take advantage of the power of compounding interest. The winner of the competition will receive a $10,000 brokerage savings account. One of the conditions of the competition is the winner may not withdraw any of that money for the first ten years. My hope is that the winner of the competition will invest the money in an index fund that returns at least 7% and doubles over the next ten years. To do that, the funds must perform as well as the historical average of the stock market at 7%. Therefore, the idea is the winner is not walking away with $10,000 but instead closer to $20,000 assuming a ten-year investment.

Here are the standings of the High School Stock Market Competition, as of April 1st:

Update: High School Stock Market Competition—April

	Name	Total	City
1.	ImShortButImLong	$12,272.98	New York, NY
2.	TheBull	$12,113.23	Seattle, WA
3.	Smootherrific	$11,958.72	St. Louis, MO
4.	DivOrDie	$11,544.53	Charlotte, NC
5.	FillOrKill	$11,432.91	San Francisco, CA

There are two weeks to go, kiddos. **I will announce the winner of the competition on April 15th after the close of the stock market.**

If you have read this newsletter, then you will understand what you need to know about the competition. You kiddos are what us old people envy. Time is on your side and not mine.

Yours truly,
Baron Wufot

Compounding Interest Fun Fact: Your money will double every 10 years at a 7% rate of return, which is the historical average return of the S&P 500 index. Your money triples after 16 years and quadruples after 20 years. An initial investment of $10,000 invested that returns 7% over 20 years will be worth nearly $40,000!

"No matter what I do, it is impossible to overtake ImShortButLong," Smooth complained at the club meeting. "That flipping leprechaun is getting on my first nerve, I'm going to kick his pot of gold over the freaking St. Louis Arch or his rainbow, whichever is easier. You know what they say?"

"Let's hear it, first nerve boy," Malibu Martin responded.

"When the tough get going, I catch a ride!" Smooth shouted. It was quite the Smootherific tantrum.

"I think you meant to say, 'when the going gets tough, the tough invest in penny stocks!'" Malibu joked.

"That's not what I said, but that is not a bad idea," Smooth told us. "Or another good saying is, 'what kills you only makes it easier.'"

"Smooth, you are on fire today," Logi said with a laugh. "I think you meant to say, 'what doesn't kill you makes you stronger.'"

"Sheesh, that's what I said!" Smooth raged. "Plus, this stupid article came out in the school newspaper and it labels me as a 'financial whiz kid' and possibly the 'nextgen Baron Wufot.' I'm neither of those things, considering that I'm now in third place behind ImShortButImLong and TheBull. I'll tell you what is TheBull, it's losing and I don't like losing, especially when it is $10,000. I have to win this competition, even if it means staying up for the final fourteen days to figure out how to beat the stock market. I will own the stock market at the end of these fourteen days and I will win the competition. Just watch!"

"So what are you thinking, guy?" Malibu Martin croaked in his froggy voice. "I would personally recommend a couple of penny stocks. This is coming from the guy who just went from the top five to the bottom five. You probably don't want my advice. You were right about penny stocks, Franklin. It's stupid to invest in companies with a ton of debt and hardly any revenue. It is a formula for disaster."

"Live and learn, that's exactly why we are participating in this competition," I said. "It's not like I'm ripping it up. Logi and I have returned about 4% in the last five months. And there's not much of a chance we are going to win it either. But my goal all along is to learn how to manage a stock portfolio."

"Now Smooth, on the other hand, he actually has a chance to win it!" Logi stated. "I wish I had the answer for you, Smooth. But at this point, I don't think it is right to voice my opinion any longer. I can only suggest that you do your homework and don't make any emotional decisions. I'm guessing almost everybody near the top will try to go big to win first place. It wouldn't be a bad idea to play it safe. Again, this is the opinion of someone who has been in the middle of the pack and heavily invested in conservative stocks."

"Buying penny stocks is a losing battle. We've learned that much," Smooth commented. "What if I sold my two worst stocks and put that money into my top returning stock, which has been Gondo Semiconductors? Gondo Semiconductors is practically the only producer of the Artificial Intelligence microchips that are spreading robots all over the solar system. The Artificial Intelligence Robots are replicating so fast, practically the only microchips being produced now are made by Gondo Semiconductors. The world has never seen anything like this!"

"Sounds like that would definitely increase your risk, which means Gondo Semiconductors could make a big move in either direction," I told him. "When does Gondo Semiconductors report earnings? Didn't Baron just get done warning us about the upcoming earnings season?"

"You're going to love this," Smooth said with a big grin on his face. "Gondo Semiconductors reports after the bell on April 14th, which means whatever the stock does during the day on April 15th would determine whether I win or lose the competition."

"Smooth, that just sounds like a horrible idea to me," I warned him. "That means everything you've done over the last six months would come down to a one-day gamble on a stock. This is your decision to make, but I don't like your odds. Just know that if you go through with this strategy, you will have a 50/50 chance of winning. This is stock speculation, or in other words: gambling. Please take a couple of days to think this through. You still have a couple of weeks until the end of the competition."

"You're right, I should take a couple of days to think about it." Smooth responded. "If I win this competition, then it may change my whole life. For starters, I would become an instant celebrity and I probably would not be able to leave the house without being swarmed by chicks. Maybe I wouldn't have to take out the trash anymore. My whole life could change!"

"Just think about all of the girls you'll be able to get, Smooth. You'll be the smoothest dude this side of the Mississippi River," Malibu Martin joked. "Girls love men with deep pockets, plus that big smooth belly of yours. You'll be a legend!"

"You two are out of control," Logi cut in. "Just one problem. Even if you win, you won't be able to access the $10,000 prize for at least ten years. Remember, that was Baron Wufot's condition for the prize money. He wants to make sure the winner learns how powerful an investment can be with compounding interest over ten years. Besides, only girls with no brains fall in love with a guy for money. Smooth, you are better than that."

"Honestly, this is the most exciting thing that has ever happened in the solar system," I partially joked. "I can't wait to see how this plays out. Dude, you got this!"

Brrrrriiiiinnnngggggg!!! Brrrrriiiiinnnngggggg!!! Brrrrriiiiinnnngggggg!!!

"We should plan on meeting after school on April 15th for the announcement of the winner of the competition," Logi suggested.

"That's a great idea. Professor Crutchfield, do you think we can get access to this classroom after school on the 15th?" I asked.

"Absolutely, don't you kids worry about it. I will see the classroom is open," Professor Crutchfield informed us.

"What time does the stock market normally close?" Malibu questioned.

"It works out perfectly. The stock market closes at 4 pm east coast time, so 3 pm central time in St. Louis. School gets out at 2:45 pm, which gives us fifteen minutes to get here and get set up for Baron Wufot's announcement."

"I'll bring the chips and salsa, if someone else will bring the orange sodie," Malibu Martin announced.

"I can bring the orange soda. Great idea," I said.

"What's a party without pork rinds! I'll bring them," Smooth added.

"I guess that leaves me, I'll make some kale chips for the party. You'll love my new recipe," Logi offered.

"Okay, that sounds delicious. At least the chips part, I don't know what to think about the kale part." Malibu Martin joked.

"Alright, I can't be late again. I'm out the door, dinosaurs," Smooth said as he stomped out of the room.

"In a shake, rattlesnake," Malibu Martin said as he slithered out of the room.

"Give a kiss, goldfish," I said as I gave Logi a kiss on the forehead and swam out of the room.

Professor Crutchfield boomed in laughter, "Hey Zeus almighty. Ha-ha-ha-ha!!!"

19

Bombing Hills

After the close of the stock market on April 14th, Gondo Semiconductors reported their quarterly numbers. The press release read:

An Earnings Miss:

Gondo Semiconductors (ticker: GOND) reported earnings of 20 cents per share, which missed the consensus estimate of 25 cents.

Lower revenues and higher expenses were the main reason for the earnings miss.

Lower than expected revenues:

GOND posted net revenues of $12.8 billion, which was below the consensus estimate of 14.5 billion.

Higher than expected expenses:

Net expenses rose 5% year over year to $8.2 billion.

After hours trading:

Following the earnings release, GOND traded down 3% in the pre-trading session. Clearly, the initial reaction of investors has been negative. We expect GOND to trade down 3-5% in tomorrow's session.

I was getting ready for work when I peeked at my phone to check Gondo's earnings numbers. The initial numbers didn't look good for Gondo Semiconductors, which could mean certain doom for Smooth. Gondo Semiconductors had been Smooth's go-to stock during the competition. It was the stock that kept Smooth in the top five of the competition and this miss could mean Smooth was out of the competition. That is, if he had gone through with his plan to sell his worst two stocks and concentrate all of his money into Gondo Semiconductors, which he most likely did. He had been secretive about his decision, but knowing Smooth, I was almost certain that he had gambled it all on Gondo Semiconductors.

To be considerate, I decided not to text Smooth. There was a good chance he was already aware of the bad news and he was probably at home beating his head against the wall, repeatedly. Besides, I had to get to work or I was going to be late.

I felt horrible. Smooth was my best friend and this was a chance for him to get ahead in life. He wasn't the sharpest tool in the shed and probably wouldn't go to college. I was hoping if he won the competition it would motivate him to give college a second thought. As his best friend, I wanted Smooth to succeed in life.

You're not going to believe what happened the next day at lunch. Smooth walked into the cafeteria with a white gauze bandage around his head and two black eyes. Yes, like a white bandage that you would get at the emergency room if you cracked open your head from beating it on the wall. He looked absolutely ridiculous with his blond, curly hair hanging out of the bandage in a big puff ball.

Smooth set his tray down and sat next to me at the lunch table.

"Dude, what happened to you? You okay?" I asked.

"I hit my noggin," Smooth replied.

"Obviously," I continued. "Does this have anything to do with Gondo Semiconductors missing their earnings numbers?"

"Gondo missed their earnings numbers?" Smooth acted surprised.

"Are you kidding me! Smooth, you had a chance to win $10,000 if Gondo Semiconductors hit their numbers and you didn't even check to see what they reported?!" I was shocked.

"Dude, I was in the hospital last night. Some things are more important than money, Franklin," Smooth said.

"I'm sorry, man. What happened? You still haven't told me," I asked.

"You see, I got this new longboard and I was out bombing hills with Malibu Martin," Smooth began to explain.

"Wait, back up," I interrupted. "You were bombing hills with Malibu Martin on a skateboard. What exactly do you mean by bombing hills? Like throwing bombs at hills while riding a skateboard? Are we talking grenades or firecrackers? That's insane, Smooth. Did you get arrested?"

"Slow down, dude, and listen to me for a second. You are currently in the process of pulling a Smooth move, says the guy with the bandage on his head and two black eyes," joked Smooth. "You see, when you bomb a hill, it just means going really fast down a steep hill on a skateboard."

"Smooth, what is wrong with you? That's equally as dumb, considering you've been skateboarding for all of one whole day. What made you think it was a good idea to go screaming down a hill? And by the looks of things, you didn't even have a helmet on. Smooth, you've got to stop and think once in a while."

"Dude, you sound like mummy. Besides, do you really think I can fit a helmet over this melon?" Smooth said. Smooth was the only person I knew who called his mom, "mummy." Like he was British or something.

"So you went skateboarding last night and decided to bomb some hills. What happened next?" I asked.

"Yeah, Malibu Martin and I were out bombing hills when all of a sudden a car came out of nowhere. Instead of t-boning the car, I dove off of my skateboard and had an unfortunate run-in with a 1980ish Slomobile XT. I can still picture that piece of junk car right before I smashed into it. That is the last thing I remember. The next thing I know, I am in the emergency room and there is dried blood all over my face and shirt. At first, I thought it might have been Halloween or something."

"Are you sure you are okay? You could have died, Smooth. Why are you even at school?" I didn't know what else to say.

"Yeah, I feel a little fuzzy, but that is nothing new," he said jokingly.

"You're lucky to be alive," I told him.

"It's really not as bad as it looks. I'm just glad I chose a junker of a car to fly headfirst into and not some fancy new autonomous car. Plus, I only had to get eight stitches this time, which brings my annual total up to twenty-two stitches. Last year by this time, I already had something like forty stitches, so that's an improvement."

"Smooth, you're not making sense. You didn't have forty stitches last year and up until this point, you haven't had any stitches this year," I said and I was starting to worry whether Smooth was alright. I was tempted to take him to the school nurse to get a second opinion.

"Oh, well it really doesn't hurt. I'm just glad you are here, Franklin," Smooth said in a daze.

"Dude, I am starting to worry that you're not so smootherific. Let's sit here and take it easy for a bit. Well, I guess that explains why you didn't catch Gondo Semi's earnings report." I said.

"Ding, ding, ding. I'm going to have to start calling you 'fast Franklin.' Dude come on, I'm the one concussed like Soda Popinski," joked Smooth. "So what happened with Gondo Semiconductors? Did I win?"

"Not if you were long the stock Gondo. They reported lower than expected earnings and revenues, plus their expenses came in higher than forecasted. Last I checked, their stock price was down 4%."

Smooth immediately jumped up out of his seat and started screaming, "I might have won! I might have won! Aroooooo-aroooooo! I still have a chance!" He caught me off guard and I thought he hadn't heard what I had said or at least did not understand the words coming out of my mouth. He just escaped death and maybe he wasn't alright. Plus, he was howling like a wolf. "Aroooo-aroooo!"

"Smooth, are you sure you are okay? Listen to me. I don't think you understand! Gondo's stock price was down 4% about an hour ago. If you are long (expect the stock to go up) Gondo Semiconductors, there is no way you can win this competition," I said as nicely as possible.

"That, my friend, is where you are wrong," Smooth shouted. "Remember when you told me I had a 50/50 chance of winning? Well, that was NOT fully accurate. It would have been accurate if I decided to sell my two worst stocks and put all of that money into Gondo Semiconductors, which was my original plan."

"Yeah, and what are you trying to tell me, Smooth?" I was lost.

"Well that night after the last meeting, I was up late doing my geometry homework, at least I was trying to do my geometry homework. You know me, I have never been that good with maps and countries. No matter, all I could think about was the stock market competition and the financial quagmire I was in."

"Wait Smooth, you just confused the word geography with geometry, which is easy to do. Then you used the word quagmire in a sentence, which is not easy to do. Are you sure they tightened all of your screws up last night at the emergency room?" I was really worried about him, but I also wanted to hear where he was going with this story. So I let him ramble on. "Okay, continue."

"I was perplexed. I went over every possible scenario in my mind but I couldn't come up with a clear solution," Smooth continued to explain. "Then, I remembered the book you let me borrow on the stock market. I think it was called *Hedge Funds Explained*. You said it would explain why that leprechaun was in first place and it would also explain why that leprechaun goes by the call name 'ImShortButImLong.' Do you remember which book I'm talking about?" Smooth questioned.

"Yeah, I know exactly what book you are talking about. Tell me you returned it to the library by now?" I asked, but I already knew what the answer was going to be.

"Don't worry, I'll bring it back tomorrow. If I win, I'll even pay the late fees on it. JOKING, I am just joking, Franklin. I'll pay the late fees no matter what." Smooth continued. "Anyway, I decided if I had a 50/50 chance to win, I should try to do the unsmooth thing by doing the exact opposite of what I thought I should do. Instead of going long by buying more shares in Gondo Semiconductors, I decided to sell all of my shares in Gondo Semiconductors. Yes, that's right, I sold all of my shares in Gondo Semiconductors! At the time, I knew it was the craziest thing I could do because Gondo Semiconductors had been my number one stock throughout the whole competition. Gondo Semiconductors was the sole reason I remained in the top five throughout the competition. But I knew I had to do the opposite of what my gut was telling me. So I just kept telling myself I had to make the unsmooth move, which meant selling all of my stock in Gondo Semiconductors."

"Smooth, you are a freaking financial wizard. A genius! Just when I thought you had gone and lost the competition, you do this! Unbelievable!" I could hardly contain myself. "I have just one question. What does that book have to do with anything?"

"In the book, *Hedge Funds Explained*, it said if I thought the stock price was going down, I should short sell the stock.

But for the life of me, I couldn't figure out what 'short selling' meant. Then, I remembered you saying 'don't worry about what short selling means, because it's too complicated for any of us to understand.' Any time you give me financial advice, Franklin, I take it and I store it in this big heart of mine. I knew I had no business trying to short sell a stock because I didn't understand what that meant. Then it occurred to me that the leprechaun, also known as 'ImShortButImLong,' had been pulling off this complicated stock strategy or maybe his dad had been helping him cheat. If he was in fact cheating by having his dad help him, in that scenario I didn't have a chance to win. On the other hand, if that freaking leprechaun had been pulling this off on his own, then my only hope was he would overplay his hand and beat himself. Mulling over these two scenarios, I decided the only thing I could do to overtake him was to basically freeze my account. To freeze my account, I sold off my riskiest stocks like Gondo Semiconductors. I reinvested the money in a conservative total market index fund. I told myself I wasn't going to beat myself this time, and all I could hope for was that tiny leprechaun would do something stupid to beat himself." Smooth was basically singing this while he moved his hands back and forth like he was a classical music conductor.

"Smooth, I barely understand what it means to short sell a stock. And you are right, it's one of the riskiest and most complicated moves to get right. You made the right move, especially considering Gondo Semiconductors was going to report their earnings right before the end of the competition," I said.

By this point in the conversation, we were starting to attract a crowd in the lunchroom. I don't know if it was Smooth's singing and dancing that drew attention to us or someone overheard he might win the stock market competition. You could see kids scurrying from table to table spreading the rumor that Smooth had won the competition, which he hadn't. You know how rumors spread in high school. It was spreading like wildfire and by the end of the day, there was no telling what the rumor would morph into.

"Piece of pie," Smooth said proudly.

"Dude, I think you meant to say 'piece of cake,' which is exactly my point," I said. "Let me get this straight. You are basically holding a hand of super conservative stocks that will most likely not go up or down. Your strategy is to let the other top investors make the mistake of gambling on risky stocks to win."

"You are exactly right, Franklin," I just didn't see any other scenario to beat them. That is unless I got lucky gambling on a stock or, alternatively, if I held tight to let them make the mistake. So instead of gambling, I decided to play it conservative with the hope that ImShortButImLong would mess up," Smooth confirmed.

"Smooth, no matter what happens, your strategy was sound. In fact, it was genius! I'm really proud of you. It takes a lot of determination and thought to learn from your mistakes and to have the vision to do this. We're all capable of changing for the better and you are living proof!" I complimented him.

20

The Power of Compounding Interest

As school let out, rumors were running wild. One kid asked me if Smooth had really won a billion dollars in the lottery. Another asked me if it was true Smooth had won the World Series of Poker. It was hilarious! The competition was far from over and Smooth had already become an instant celebrity at St. Louis High School. You gotta love a good high school rumor!

When I showed up to room #244, where we normally met for the club, it was overflowing with kids. It was unreal! I hardly knew any of the other students. It appeared the whole school was there to see if Smooth had won the competition.

Professor Crutchfield made his way to the doorway of room #244 and made the announcement he had opened up the big auditorium so we could all hear Baron Wufot's announcement. So the mass of students slowly migrated to the big auditorium for the conference call.

As advertised, the call started promptly at 3 pm. But since we moved the meeting into the big auditorium, we were a little unprepared for the call. I put my cell phone on speakerphone mode and then I laid a microphone from the auditorium's PA system next to my cell phone to amplify the call. It wasn't pretty, but it worked.

Tap, tap, tap, tap, tap, tap

"Tater, is this thing on?" Baron Wufot said to the universe.

"Yes, Mr. Wufot. You are live to the world," said Tater.

"Thanks, Tate Dog! Um, yeah, Tater, can you grab me a Diet Dr. Pep and some carrot sticks," Baron asked Tater. It was obvious the Baron didn't care who was listening. The Baron continued. "Now, for the moment we have all been waiting for. It has been an exciting six months and it is an honor to announce the winner of the first-ever High School Stock Market Competition.

But before I lose your attention, I would like to tell you a quick story about my childhood. Here it goes!

When I was a wee boy growing up in Jefferson City, Missouri, all I ever wanted was to be rich. All I could think about was money and how I was going to make my next dollar. So at the age of twelve, I went down to the local newspaper's office and asked for a job. There were laws against children working at this young age, but I wasn't going to let that keep me from my dream of becoming rich. The editor of the newspaper was no dummy and he immediately asked me my age. Without hesitation, I told him I was fourteen years old, which was the legal working age at the time. The editor winked at me and said he just fired his third delivery boy of the month. He was in a bind and would try me out for a month. He told me if I could do a good job and be on time, the job would be mine going forward. That was my first job, and from that day on I have had at least one job. The last I checked, I am eighty-two years old, so that means I have been working for seventy years now. Whoa, that is unbelievable!

Tater Higgins! I'm old and I need a Diet Dr. Pep to wet my whistle. Make that ASAP, my fine man. Like today. I need to take my vitamins!

Sorry about that, kiddos. Every man needs a Diet Dr. Pep at least five times a day and I think Tater Higgins is withholding an icy cold beverage from me. Um, yeah. Where was I? That's right, I'm old and I have been working over seventy years now.

Early in my career, I worked hard. It wasn't out of the ordinary for me to have two or three jobs at once. During those early years, I figured I was just trading hours for money. If I worked for one hour at $1.50, I made $1.50. If I worked two hours delivering newspapers, I made $3.00.

It wasn't long before I realized there weren't enough hours in the day to make me as rich as I wanted to be. So, I had a problem. I could either continue to work myself into the ground or I could find a solution to getting rich. That's when I discovered the library. Every free minute I had, I would spend it at the public library in Jeff City, MO. I like to joke that the library made me rich. But as I got older, I came to realize the library not only made me rich, it also taught me how to learn. The most important thing I learned is that learning is the key to happiness. If you are a happy learner, then it is a lot easier to achieve your goal. I was driven to learn. Money just happened to be what I was passionate about. I discovered it is learning that makes me happy. Fortunately, a by-product of learning was that now I had discovered the formula for making money. I've always been greedy for learning new things, not money.

At the library, I learned about the difference between 'active income' and 'passive income.' This discovery is what changed the rest of my life. Learning the difference between passive income and active income is what made me the richest man in the world. The discovery of passive income, in addition to the discovery of compounding interest, was the secret to accumulating wealth. Both are equally important, especially for young adults. Active income is when you trade hours worked for money. That is the type of income I had been earning up 'til that point in my life.

Passive income is when you can make your money work for you. That means while you are sleeping, your money is still at work making more money for you. Yeah, that is right, you can make money while you are sleeping! An example would be investing in the stock market. If you invest $1,000 at sixteen years old and it returns the historical average of 7%, at the age of sixty years old, you will have $21,564 at retirement. That means you made a profit of $20,564 off of your initial $1,000.

Given:

    Starting Value: $1,000
    Monthly contribution: $0
    Time: 44 yrs to retirement
    Savings rate: 7% (historical market average is 7%)
    Value at Retirement: $21,564

With the power of passive income and compounding interest, nearly everyone can grow a vast amount of wealth if you start saving early enough. The stock market is a great example of putting your money to work for you in the form of passive income.

Passive income can be loosely defined as putting your money to work for you while you are hunting zzz's. What are some other examples of passive income? Off the top of my bald ole head, here are the ones that come to mind: investing in real estate, writing a book, blogging, developing an app, creating an online store, putting money into index funds, renting out your closet space, owning your own business, recording music to sell, and lastly, how about becoming a fashion designer. All of these qualify as passive income. Like most things in life, you just have to dream it and then figure out how to do it. Take my word for it, you will probably have to work for a large portion of your life. The sooner you start developing your own passive income streams, the easier your financial life will become.

Once I came across the idea of passive income at the library, it started to make sense to me how individuals could accumulate large amounts of wealth. My only problem was, I was money poor and time rich. So I did the one thing I knew how to do. I went to the library to learn about investing in the stock market. Later on down the road, I started to learn about real estate investing.

Every day after work, I went to the library to study how the stock market worked. I read every finance book I could get my hands on. When I ran out of finance books that focused on the stock market, I switched to reading personal finance books that taught me how to manage and save more of the money I was making.

Eventually, I slowly began to buy individual stocks. At first, I was horrible at it. I had a knack for choosing the wrong stocks to invest in. But I didn't give up. When you don't have a lot of money, you don't have a lot of money to lose. It is about the only time in your life when it pays not to have a lot of money in your bank account. I always say, 'learn with a little.' I was young when I started investing, probably seventeen or eighteen years old. At that point, I barely had enough money to even open a brokerage account, which played to my advantage. If you 'learn with a little,' you can afford to take chances and to learn from your mistakes. If you lose 10% of $100, then you've only lost $10. If you lose 10% of $1,000, then you have only lost $100. Now, if you lose 10% of $1,000,000, then you have lost $100,000. You see how it pays to 'learn with a little'? Make your mistakes when the stakes are low. Then down the road when the stakes are higher, you will have more experience to base your decisions on.

Another thing I've thought a lot about over the years is that learning to invest is the best investment you can make. Learning to invest on your own is cheaper than just about any college class you can take at a university. Not only is it cheaper, but as you learn to invest you actually start making passive income off of your investments. Therefore, any small amount of money you lose in the beginning will be paid for with returns from future investments. It is normal for a college student to graduate with thirty or forty thousand dollars in student loan debt. What is debt doing for you? Nothing! Is it making money for you? No! Most recent graduates do not understand how investing money in the stock market works, because they are so far in debt they feel handcuffed. They don't want to take a chance of learning about the stock market or real estate. So instead, they enter the 'active income' workforce, which means their income is solely based on how many hours they can work. By getting a job with a salary, they are rewarded even less for working longer hours. It's even worse than active income because when you get paid a salary or a fixed dollar amount, it doesn't reward you for working extra hours. This is what they call the rat race: an endless pursuit that offers little reward or purpose. Others might call it being on a hamster wheel because you are stuck in an endless cycle between going to work and being at home with little reward.

Take my word, kiddos, you don't want to enter the rat race. At this point in your life, you are in the position to choose your destiny. It will never be easier because you have no debt and very few expenses. You don't have to pay for housing, utilities, food, etc. Take advantage of this and go get a job. Even if you are only working a few hours a week, you will learn valuable money lessons that will last a lifetime.

Um, yeah, sorry I got a little sidetracked. Where was I? Oh yeah, after a couple years of making mistakes in the stock market, mainly due to being too aggressive, I got tired of losing money. I refocused all of my efforts on discovering how companies make a good investment.

I learned that if I could invest in undervalued companies with a proven track record, they would slowly increase in value over time. Another important thing I learned is the longer I could hold a stock, the more my money would grow without having to lift a finger. Investing in undervalued growth companies and having patience made me the richest man in the world. Kiddos, it is important for you to understand, time and compounding interest will make you richer than your wildest dreams.

Eventually, I stopped seeing dollar signs and over time it became about winning. Investing became a competition I wanted to win, which meant having the highest score. Investing in the stock market is kind of like being a good fisherman. Once you have honed your skills and learned how to catch the big fish, it doesn't mean you don't get excited when you catch another big fish. And no matter how many big fish you catch, you still get excited when you catch another. For me, making an investment in an undervalued growth stock and then watching it grow never gets old for me. To this day, I still get excited when a stock hits an inflection point and races off to accumulate massive returns.

The point is, if you want to live a rich life, then live your life to learn. Figure out your passions and learn everything you can. Make that passion your life purpose. Even if investing in the stock market is not your first passion, it is worth your time to learn about it. By investing and saving money, you will break free from an 'active income' lifestyle and eventually reach financial independence. You will feel enabled to do and learn whatever makes you happy. Life is most definitely not all about money. Life is about purpose. About learning and working towards that purpose in life.

What sucked me into investing in the stock market is that it offers an unlimited amount of opportunities to learn. The more you learn about the stock market, the better an investor you will become. The end result: you earn more money. Once you become a better investor, your money will grow. Then one day you reach the ultimate achievement of financial independence. Reaching financial independence means you are not dependent on money any longer and you can do exactly what you want, when you want to do it. The way I like to think about it is that you can learn whatever you want to learn, when you want to learn it.

Okay, well um. That just about covers everything I had written down on my napkin.

TATER, WHERE IS THAT DIET DR. PEP!!??
I NEED TO TAKE MY VITAMINS!!!

Now, for the moment you have all been waiting for. I'm going to start with the fifth place winner. Initially, I had not planned on awarding prizes to any of the other places. Over the past six months, it became more and more apparent to me that a lot of hard work was going into this competition. Therefore, I have decided to reward the top five finishers. That's right, I am going to award prizes to all of the top five finishers.

In fifth place and the winner of a $500 brokerage account. Drum roll please…the fifth place winner is DivOrDie from Charlotte, NC! With a name like that, I expect you will become a dividend investor for many years to come. I'm guessing DivOrDie stands for Dividends or Die. Oh and by the way, your $500 award will be worth about $10,782 in 44 years, if you can keep it invested until retirement.

Remember kiddos, if you want to find the Future Value or the Value at Retirement, all you have to do is enter the following numbers in your compound interest calculator or app:

Starting Value: $500
Monthly contribution: $0
Time: 44 yrs to retirement
Savings rate: 7% (historical market average is 7%)
Value at Retirement: $10,782

I always assume the stock market's historical average rate of return of 7% when I do compounding interest calculations like this. Since the 1940s, the market has returned over 7% on average per year. The lesson to learn here is to put your money in a secure investment like a total market index fund and let it ride until you absolutely need it. Now even better, if you contribute a measly $100 a month for 44 years to that initial investment of $500, you will have roughly $363,000 at retirement. Again, for you kiddos using a compound interest app on your phone, enter the following numbers to find the value at retirement:

Starting Value: $500
Monthly contribution: **$100**
Time: 44 yrs to retirement
Savings rate: 7% (historical market average is 7%)
Value at Retirement: $363,000

That's right! By investing only $100 a month, you can be into the six figures easily by retirement. Further, if you contribute $200 a month to that brokerage account, your money will compound to over $715,000 by retirement.

Yes, you heard me correctly. If you contribute $200 a month, you can have over $700,000 in your brokerage savings account at retirement.

Now, some good news for everybody that did not finish in the top five of the competition. If you contribute $100 a month to an an index fund that returns an average return of 7% a year for 44 years, you will have $352,000 in that retirement account.

Notice, the amount is only $10,000 less than the fifth

place finisher that won $500. The point I am making is: **you are all winners if you start investing now, in your teens. Each and every one of you can retire wealthy by saving as little as $100.**

Now for you kiddos starting from scratch, if you save $200 a month for the next 44 years at a 7% rate of return, you will have earned $705,000 at retirement.

If you are capable and somewhat motivated, you have no excuse not to start saving immediately. Now is the time to start saving, not in ten or twenty or thirty years from now. For example, take note of this. This is the power of compounding interest over long periods of time:

» A 16-year-old invests $200 per month for **44** years at 7% = **$705,070** at retirement

» A 26-year-old invests $200 per month for **34** years at 7% = **$333,615** at retirement

» A 36-year-old invests $200 per month for **24** years at 7% = **$148,780** at retirement

» A 46-year-old invests $200 per month for **14** years at 7% = **$56,807** at retirement

What's the only variable that changes in this example? It's the length of time the same amount of money was invested.

And yes kiddos, I did all of those calculations in my head. Not bad for an eighty-year-old man! Isn't it amazing how much more money you can accumulate if you start putting compounding interest to work as early as in your teens?

Now, on to our fourth-place finisher, who will receive a brokerage account containing $1,000. Yes, you heard me right! The fourth place finisher will be receiving a brokerage account with $1,000. Fourth place goes to TheBull from Seattle, Washington. Congratulations to TheBull!

Now, let's look at how TheBull can put that money to work. That $1,000 invested for 44 years at an average rate of return of 7% will be worth $21,564 at retirement. If you are able to contribute a measly $100 a month to that initial investment of $1,000, you will have $374,000 by retirement. I just love saying the words, 'if you save a mere $100 a month…, you will have over $374,000.' It feels so good coming out of my mouth! Now, if TheBull contributes $200 a month until retirement, he or she will have $726,635 saved up for retirement. What's crazy about this is even if you don't start out with an initial investment of $1,000, but start from zero all you have to do is save $200 a month and you will have $705,000 saved for retirement. The initial investment of $1,000 does help, but it is not that big of a game changer. Start saving, kiddos!

I hope you all are getting as excited as I am by all of this talk of compounding interest. You kiddos may think I'm crazy, but by discovering passive income and compounding interest I have become the richest man in the world. Granted, there was luck involved along the way, but wealth is the result of learning and dedication. You kiddos can retire wealthy just by saving a hundred dollars a month. Just remember, it just takes a little discipline in your early years.

The third-place finisher and the winner of a $2,000 brokerage account goes to SmallCapWonder from New York, NY. I love that name, SmallCapWonder, and judging from your holdings you have done an awesome job managing a portfolio full of small companies. Not an easy thing to do, but it can be a very profitable investment strategy if you can successfully invest in small capitalization stocks. And now for the fun part. That $2,000 funded brokerage account SmallCapWonder just won will be worth roughly $43,000 if invested in a fund that returns the historical market average of 7% over the next 44 years until retirement. That means for every $2,000 invested at the age of sixteen, you should make a profit of $41,000! If SmallCapWonder is able to contribute $100 per month, you will have roughly $395,000 at retirement. With a $200 monthly contribution, SmallCapWonder will have saved roughly $750,000!

I hope all of you are starting to realize, you must start early and continue to save in the long term in order to accumulate wealth. By saving as little as a hundred or two hundred dollars a month, you can achieve financial freedom when you are young enough to enjoy it! Today, there are five winners fortunate enough to get a little head start. But the rest of you are winners, too! By listening to this broadcast, a financial seed has been planted and many of you will have already begun your financial journey.

TATER! DIET DR. PEP PLEASE! I NEED TO TAKE MY VITAMINS!

It's getting hot in here! That leaves us with two winners to announce. The second place award and the winner of a $5,000 funded brokerage account is Smootherrific from St. Louis, Misery. Ha-ha-ha kiddos, I'm just joking. Take my word for it, I would not be living in Missouri if I wasn't totally in love with the state. There are a lot of things that contribute to a happy life and where you live is definitely a factor in that equation.

Smootherrific is a stone-cold investor. He jumped out to an early lead and he remained in the top five throughout the whole competition. You should be proud of yourself, kiddo. If the past six months are any indication of your investment style, you are on the road to financial freedom! By the way, are you really that smooth?

Now, for my favorite part. Smootherrific, if you are smooth enough to invest an additional $100 a month to the initial investment of $5,000, you will have roughly $460,000 at retirement. If you are able to smoothly contribute $200 a month to your brokerage investment account, then you will have roughly $810,000 at retirement."

The auditorium erupted when Smooth's name was announced as the second-place finisher of a $5,000 brokerage account. He defied all odds and pulled off the unthinkable. He truly did pull a Smooth move. Smooth jumped up on the stage in the auditorium and started beating his chest like King Kong on top of the Empire State Building. I did my best to keep everyone from tackling him. By this point, Smooth's white gauze bandage around his head had been almost completely unraveled and his two black eyes had turned an even darker shade. Smooth resembled a Moroccan Berber that had fallen off his camel. He was in rough shape. His head was partially shaved where he had gotten stitches and the rest of his head was still overflowing with puffs of blond curls. Smooth looked more like he had won the Royal Rumble instead of a stock market competition. Or as Smooth would say, the "thrilla of vanilla!"

Baron Wufot's call continued…

"...and the winner of the $10,000 brokerage account goes to ImShortButImLong from New York! Kiddo, you and Smootherrific have been battling it out throughout the whole competition. You've got some huevos to stick to your investment strategy. You trade stocks like you are a pro and I expect big things out of you for years to come. Now, for my favorite part. That $10,000 you just won will be worth over $215,000 at retirement if you save for the next 44 years and keep it invested in an index fund that returns the historical market average of 7%. If you are as motivated as I think you are and find a way to contribute $100 monthly to the account until retirement, you will have over $560,000 in that account. A monthly contribution of $200 will compound to be worth over $920,000. With a little discipline and a lot of patience, kiddo, you are on your way to financial independence.

FINAL RESULTS: High School Stock Market Competition

	Name	Total	City
1.	ImShortButImLong	$12,272.98	New York, NY
2.	Smootherrific	$11,958.72	St. Louis, MO
3.	SmallCapWonder	$11,517.34	New York, NY
4.	TheBull	$12,113.23	Seattle, WA
5.	DivOrDie	$11,544.53	Charlotte, NC

I would like to congratulate all of the participants in the first annual Baron Wufot's High School Stock Market Competition. You can all be winners by starting to save as little as $100 a month and continuing to educate yourself on personal finance.

Again, I would like to remind the top five winners, you will not be able to withdraw any of your money for the initial ten years. The idea is to invest the award money in a vehicle like an index fund. You will double your money in ten years and most likely, you will continue to grow the investment until retirement.

Before I sign off, I have one last award to give out. One young kiddo showed great courage and innovation by contacting me with the idea of starting this competition. A kiddo by the name of Franklin Fi proposed the idea of this stock market challenge. Immediately, I fell in love with the idea and realized the value in this type of competition. I immediately realized, if organized properly, I could use the competition as a tool to spread my knowledge of personal finance and investment strategy to your generation. My newsletter planted the seed, but this competition is the wind that will blow personal finance seeds to students all over the country.

To thank this Mr. Franklin Fi, I would like to reward him with a summer internship at the international headquarters of Baron Wufot Inc. in Jefferson City, MO. My vision is to team up with Franklin Fi in order to plant more personal finance seeds and to reach even more of your generation. I have always surrounded myself with the brightest minds in the country and I would love for Franklin Fi to come to Baron Wufot Inc. to collaborate with me on some future projects."

The room erupted again! Everyone in the auditorium lost it. Some were chanting "Smoothtastic the Fantastic!" Others were chanting my name, "Franklin, Franklin, Franklin!" It was pure mayhem. Malibu Martin, Professor Crutchfield (yes, Professor Crutchfield was even losing his mind), along with the others boosted us up on their shoulders and proceeded to carry us through the hallway while our classmates chanted our names.

Smoothtastic the Fantastic! FRANKLIN! FRANKLIN! FRANKLIN! Smoothtastic the Fantastic! FRANKLIN! FRANKLIN! FRANKLIN! Smoothtastic the Fantastic!...

Was this another dream? Was I really just asleep again in Mr. Heartwood's biology class? I waited for the ceiling to open up and for hundred-dollar bills to rain down. But they never did. I fantasized a bright red sports car waiting for us outside. But that didn't happen either. For a moment, I was certain rappers with gold chains were going to step out and start rapping about how rich I was.

But, waiting for me outside was my and Logi's bicycles in the bike rack. This was really happening. I had just won an internship at Baron Wufot Inc., and this summer I was going to be working for the richest man in the solar system.

This was definitely not a dream. It was even better than a dream. It was the greatest day of my life, and I was a legend to all of the kids at St. Louis High!

Logi and I then hopped on our bikes and rode into the beautiful setting sun of Misery.

THE END

Epilogue

The school year was winding down and we were all starting to get excited about our summer adventures.

Smooth had landed a job working as a plumber for his uncle. It wasn't a glamorous job, but Smooth was going to make $10 an hour, which meant he was going to be making about $300 a week after taxes or roughly $3,000 for the summer.

Smooth proposed a bet of $100 he could save more money than me over the course of the summer. I didn't like the bet because I knew that Smooth was probably going to work more hours than me, possibly getting paid more per hour, and could be working fifteen to twenty hours of overtime per week, which meant that he would be getting paid time and a half for his overtime work. There was no way I could flat out earn more than Smooth over the summer. Unfortunately, we were both still "active income" earners, trading hours worked for money.

I knew I couldn't out-earn him, so I proposed we change the bet to $100 to the person with the highest savings rate. For example, if Smooth earned $3,000 over the summer and spent $2,000 throughout the summer, his savings rate would be 33%. If I earned $2,000 over the summer and saved $1,000, my savings rate would be 50% and I would be the winner. This change in the bet would put us on an equal playing field and give me a chance of winning. A long-established, personal rule is not to enter into a bet or play a game I can't win.

Smooth loved the idea and we shook on the bet. Besides putting us on an equal playing field, the change in the rules gave us and added incentive to watch our spending and save more throughout the summer.

Per usual, Malibu Martin was going to be spending his summer in Malibu, California with his grandparents. The city of Malibu is located just outside of Los Angeles and a lot of the LA celebrities have homes there. Malibu Martin loves fashion and the city of Malibu is a perfect place for him to keep his finger on the pulse of fashion.

Malibu Martin's goal for the summer was to continue to grow his vlog's followers and to network with up-and-coming fashion designers. He just bought a new camera with a huge lens to enable him to shoot street fashion discreetly without being noticed. He had also landed some press credentials for some of the LA fashion shows happening throughout the summer.

I was really proud of Malibu Martin for having the drive and vision to stick with filming his vlog. He was the only seventeen-year-old I knew with his own vlog and many followers already established. Knowing Malibu Martin, it was only a matter of time before the vlog became viral. He is a hustler and this vlog was the perfect platform for him to showcase his skills.

Logi had decided to spend another summer with her extended family in India. Last summer, she studied yoga in India and her plan was to go back to continue her training with her yoga guru.

I was definitely going to miss her, but I had no right to complain. I was going to be working in Jefferson City, MO for Baron Wufot. Logi and I had been friends a long time and I completely trusted her, as a boyfriend and a friend. We were an item now, but more importantly, we would always be really good friends. There was still that dowry thing, but Logi reassured me, she was a modern woman and wouldn't be promised to some prince of India. Maybe I was blinded by love, but I couldn't see Logi with anybody else. I knew it was going to be a long summer without her, but our affection for each other would only grow stronger with distance. I was certain of it!

As for me, I was spending the summer working at the international headquarters of Baron Wufot Inc. in Jefferson City, Missouri. Jeff City is the capital of Missouri and is about an hour and a half west of St. Louis. Fortunately, my Aunt Patty and Uncle Tom live there with my two cousins, Jarod and Kiley. Cuzin Jarod is a year older than me and just graduated from high school. He'll be going to the University of Missouri next year. Cuzin Kiley just finished her freshman year of high school. She's a lot like me in that she is constantly thinking about how to make her life happier and use that advantage to succeed in the business world. She's definitely an old soul.

My aunt and uncle have a huge house and they told me I would even have my own bedroom for the summer. Until this point in life, I have always shared a bedroom with my two brothers. It was going to be cool to finally have my own bedroom, even if it was just for the summer.

As for preparing for my internship, I took Baron Wufot's advice about spending every free minute at the library to learn about the stock market and personal finance. The last couple of weeks of school, in my free time, I was either at work at the Paddle Department Store or studying at the library. I was doing everything possible to prepare for my internship, which could lay the groundwork for becoming a stock broker. Logi understood.

At the library, I started by reading *The Intelligent Investor* by Benjamin Graham. It was recommended to me multiple times. Once I read it, I was hooked on books by Benjamin Graham. I think I scanned three or four other books by him before finally moving onto the *Rich Dad Poor Dad* series by Robert T. Kiyosaki. There are twelve books in the series. I learned to skim through one of them a night, telling myself I could always go back and read them more carefully. I wanted to consume as much information as possible on personal finance before my internship. Baron Wufot always emphasized the importance of personal finance, so I wanted to make sure I was well-versed on the subject. Next, I read *Liar's Poker* by Michael Lewis. It was another recommended book and it did not disappoint.

Each morning, I would read the *Wall Street Journal* and *Investor's Business Daily* to stay current on what was happening in the market. It didn't take long for me to realize I was out of my league, but I was trying my best to learn the basics before my internship started.

Also to prepare for my internship, I bought my very first business suit. I hesitantly used some of the money I made from my job at Paddle Department Store to buy my first suit from the Stockbroker's Warehouse, a store that specializes in business suits. It was hard to part with my hard-earned cash, but I knew I had to do it.

In spite of all my preparations, I knew there really wasn't anything I could do to be ready for what I was about to experience. I was a seventeen-year-old kid going to work for the richest man in the solar system. No matter what happened over the next couple of months, this was going to be a life-changing experience. All I could do was approach each and every day with a smile and the willingness to learn. I, Franklin Fi, was chasing my dream and for once in my life, I felt like my life's journey was starting to have a purpose.

Franklin Fi's Financials

Savings by Month

Dec	$226.07
Jan	$717.76
Feb	$1,177.97
Mar	$1,575.22
Apr	$1,972.74
May	$2,364.48

Average Savings Rate

Average from Dec to May (6 months) = 63%

By individual months…

Dec. 1—Financial Results for Franklin Fi

Total Income − Total Expenses = Profit

Profit: $393.19 − $167.12 = **$226.07**

Profit ÷ Total Income = Savings Rate

Savings Rate: $226.07 ÷ $393.19 = **57.50%**

Total Net Worth: $226.07

Jan. 1—Financial Results for Franklin Fi
Total Income − Total Expenses = Profit
Profit: $768.45 − $277.89 = **$490.56**

Profit ÷ Total Income = Savings Rate
Savings Rate: $490.56 ÷ $768.45 = **63.84%**

Total Net Worth: $226.07 + $490.56 = **$716.63**

Feb. 1—Financial Results for Franklin Fi
Total Income − Total Expenses = Profit
Profit: $689.09 − $232.47 = **$456.62**

Profit ÷ Total Income = Savings Rate
Savings Rate: $456.62 ÷ $689.09 = **66.26%**

Total Net Worth: $716.63 + $456.62 = **$1,173.25**

Mar. 1—Financial Results for Franklin Fi
Total Income − Total Expenses = Profit
Profit: $617.23 − $225.87 = **$391.36**

Profit ÷ Total Income = Savings Rate
Savings Rate: $391.36 ÷ $617.23 = **63.41%**

Total Net Worth: $1,173.25 + $391.36 = **$1,564.61**

Apr. 1—Financial Results for Franklin Fi
Total Income − Total Expenses = Profit
Profit: $604.98 − $215.34 = **$389.64**

Profit ÷ Total Income = Savings Rate
Savings Rate: $389.64 ÷ $604.98 = **64.41%**

Total Net Worth: $1,564.61 + $389.64 = **$1,954.25**

<u>May 1—Financial Results for Franklin Fi</u>

Total Income − Total Expenses = Profit

Profit: $607.82 − $225.95 = **$381.87**

Profit ÷ Total Income = Savings Rate

Savings Rate: $381.87 ÷ $607.82 = **62.83%**

Total Net Worth: $1,954.25 + $381.87 = $2,336.12

Franklin Fi's financial journey
will continue in Book 2!
Stay tuned...

Glossary of Financial Terms

Asset

An asset is a resource with economic value that an individual, corporation, or country owns or controls with the expectation that it will provide a future benefit. Assets are reported on a company's balance sheet and are bought or created to increase a firm's value or benefit the firm's operations. An asset can be thought of as something that, in the future, can generate cash flow, reduce expenses, or improve sales, regardless of whether it's manufacturing equipment or a patent.

Bond

A bond is a fixed income instrument that represents a loan made by an investor to a borrower (typically corporate or governmental). A bond could be thought of as an I.O.U. between the lender and borrower that includes the details of the loan and its payments. A bond has an end date when the principal of the loan is due to be paid to the bond owner and usually includes the terms for variable or fixed interest payments that will be made by the borrower. Bonds are used by companies, municipalities, states, and sovereign governments to finance projects and operations. Owners of bonds are debtholders, or creditors, of the issuer.

Brokerage Account

A brokerage account is an arrangement between an investor and a licensed brokerage firm permitting the investor to deposit funds with the firm and place investment orders through the brokerage. The investor owns the assets contained in the brokerage account and must usually claim as taxable income any capital gains he incurs from the account.

Compound Interest

Compound interest (or compounding interest) is interest calculated on the initial principal and that also includes all of the accumulated interest of previous periods of a deposit or loan. Thought to have originated in 17th century Italy, compound interest can be thought of as "interest on interest," and will make a sum grow at a faster rate than simple interest, which is calculated only on the principal amount. The rate at which compound interest accrues depends on the frequency of compounding such that the higher the number of compounding periods, the greater the compound interest. Thus, the amount of compound interest accrued on $100 compounded at 10% annually will be lower than that on $100 compounded at 5% semi-annually over the same time period. Because the interest-on-interest effect can generate increasingly positive returns based on the initial principal amount, it has sometimes been referred to as the "miracle of compound interest."

Dollar Cost Averaging

Dollar cost averaging refers to the process of buying (irrespective of share price) a fixed dollar amount of a particular investment on a periodic, regular schedule. Because the dollar amount does not change, the result is fewer shares being purchased when prices are high, and more shares purchased when prices are low. Over time, the cost per share tends to average out. Through this process, an investor reduces his or her risk of investing a large amount in a single investment at the wrong time.

Earnings Season

Earnings season refers to the months of the year during which most quarterly corporate earnings are released to the public. Earnings season generally occurs in the months immediately following the end of each fiscal quarter. This means that earnings seasons fall in January, April, July, and October. These lagging dates are due to the pause between when quarter-end periods and the time in which firms are able to release their earnings following their accounting periods.

Financial Statements

Financial statements are written records that convey the financial activities and conditions of a business or entity and consist of four major components. Financial statements are meant to present the financial information of the entity in question as clearly and concisely as possible for both the entity and the readers. Financial statements for businesses usually include income statements, balance sheets, statements of retained earnings, and cash flows but may also require additional detailed disclosures depending on the relevant accounting framework. Financial statements are often audited by government agencies, accountants, firms, etc. to ensure accuracy and for tax, financing, or investing purposes.

Income Statement (aka Profit and Loss Statement)

An income statement is one of the three important financial statements used for reporting a company's financial performance over a specific accounting period, with the other two key statements being the balance sheet and the statement of cash flows. Also known as the profit and loss statement or the statement of revenue and expense, the income statement primarily focuses on company's revenues and expenses during a particular period.

Index Fund

An index fund is a type of mutual fund with a portfolio constructed to match or track the components of a market index, such as the Standard & Poor's 500 index (S&P 500). An index mutual fund is said to provide broad market exposure, low operating expenses, and low portfolio turnover. These funds adhere to specific rules or standards (e.g. efficient tax management or reducing tracking errors) that stay in place no matter the state of the markets.

Long a Stock

A long (or long position) is the buying of a security such as a stock, commodity, or currency with the expectation that the asset will rise in value. In the context of options, long is the buying of an options contract. An investor that expects an asset's price to fall will go long on a put option, and an investor that hopes to benefit from an upward price movement will be long a call option.

Mutual Fund

A mutual fund is an investment vehicle made up of a pool of money collected from many investors for the purpose of investing in securities such as stocks, bonds, money market instruments, and other assets. Mutual funds are operated by professional money managers, who allocate the fund's investments and attempt to produce capital gains and/or income for the fund's investors. A mutual fund's portfolio is structured and maintained to match the investment objectives stated in its prospectus.

Net Profit Margin

Net profit margin, or net margin, is equal to net income or profits divided by total revenue, and represents how much profit each dollar of sales generates. Net profit margin is the ratio of net profits or net income to revenues for a company, business segment, or product. Net profit margin is typically expressed as a percentage but can also be represented in decimal form. The net profit margin illustrates how much of each dollar collected by a company as revenue translates into profit. The term "net profits" is equivalent to "net income" on the income statement, and one can use the terms interchangeably. Most commonly, investors will refer to net profit margin as the "net margin" and describe it as "net income" divided by total sales instead of using the term "net profits."

Personal Savings Rate

The savings rate is the ratio of personal savings to disposable personal income and can be calculated for an economy as a whole or at the personal level. The Federal Reserve defines disposable income as all sources of income minus the tax you pay on that income. Your savings is disposable income minus expenditures, such as credit card payments and utility bills. Using this approach, if you have $30,000 left over after taxes (disposable income) and spend $24,000 in expenditures, then your savings are $6,000. Dividing savings by your disposable income yields a savings rate of 20% ($6,000 ÷ $30,000 × 100).

Price-to-Earnings Ratio
The price-earnings ratio (P/E ratio) is the ratio for valuing a company that measures its current share price relative to its per-share earnings. The price-earnings ratio is also sometimes known as the price multiple or the earnings multiple.

Profit and Loss Statement
The profit and loss statement is a financial statement that summarizes the revenues, costs, and expenses incurred during a specified period, usually a fiscal quarter or year. These records provide information about a company's ability or inability to generate profit by increasing revenue, reducing costs, or both. Some refer to the P&L statement as a statement of profit and loss, income statement, statement of operations, statement of financial results or income, earnings statement, and expense statement.

Short Selling a Stock
Short selling is the sale of a security that the seller has borrowed. A short seller profits if a security's price declines. In other words, the trader sells to open the position and expects to buy it back later at a lower price and will keep the difference as a gain. Short selling may be prompted by speculation, or by the desire to hedge the downside risk of a long position in

the same security or a related one. Since the risk of loss on a short sale is theoretically unlimited, short selling should only be done by experienced traders who are familiar with the risks.

Stock

A stock (also known as "shares" and "equity") is a type of security that signifies ownership in a corporation and represents a claim on part of the corporation's assets and earnings. There are two main types of stock: common and preferred. Common stock usually entitles the owner to vote at shareholders' meetings and to receive dividends. Preferred stockholders generally do not have voting rights, though they have a higher claim on assets and earnings than the common stockholders. For example, owners of preferred stock receive dividends before common shareholders and have priority in the event that a company goes bankrupt and is liquidated.

Stockbroker

A stockbroker (also known as a registered representative, investment adviser or, simply, broker) is a professional individual who executes buy and sell orders on behalf of clients for stocks and other securities in a listed market or over the counter, usually for a fee or commission. Stockbrokers are usually associated with a brokerage firm and handle transactions for retail and institutional customers alike. Brokerage firms and broker-dealers are also sometimes referred to as stockbrokers themselves.

Stock Market Index

A market index is a weighted average of several stocks or other investment vehicles from a section of the stock market, and it is calculated from the price of the selected stocks. Market indexes are intended to represent an entire stock market and track the market's changes over time. Index values help investors track changes in market values over long periods of time. For example, the widely used Standard and Poor's 500 index is computed by combining 500 large-cap U.S. stocks into one index value. Investors can track changes in the index's value over time and use it as a benchmark for their own portfolio returns.

About the Author

Author Shane Dillon wrote *The Franklin Fi Series* while bicycling across Europe, laying the groundwork in Spain and reaching the conclusion near the Black Sea in Romania. Shane is in the constant pursuit of adventure. Over the last two years, he has ridden his trusty bicycle, Disco, across the United States and twelve countries in Europe. Yes, the name of his bike is Disco. He came up with the name Disco as a joke. Most people think of going to a bar or discoteca as fun, whereas Shane thinks cycling across a country is fun.

Shane Dillon has a degree in finance from the University of Missouri, an MBA from Sonoma State University, specializing in the Wine Industry, and twenty years of stock market experience. He hopes this story of financial freedom will inspire the next generation of bike-riding, yoga-loving, world travelers to dive deeper into the world of investment leading to a future of financial freedom.

Currently, Shane lives in Malaga, Spain and is fulfilling his dream of living abroad. During the week he writes and on the weekends he adventures throughout Europe.